D1435841

AMERICAN Underdog

AMERICAN
Underdog

HISTORIC OUTSIDER UPSET:
Ethics and Economics Matter
in Washington, DC

Congressman
DAVID BRAT

CENTER
STREET®

New York   Boston   Nashville

Copyright © 2016 by David Brat

Cover design by Dale Fiorillo
Cover photo by Vincent Remini
Cover copyright © 2016 by Hachette Book Group, Inc.

Hachette Book Group supports the right to free expression and the value of copyright. The purpose of copyright is to encourage writers and artists to produce the creative works that enrich our culture.

The scanning, uploading, and distribution of this book without permission is a theft of the author's intellectual property. If you would like permission to use material from the book (other than for review purposes), please contact permissions@hbgusa.com. Thank you for your support of the author's rights.

Center Street
Hachette Book Group
1290 Avenue of the Americas, New York, NY 10104
centerstreet.com
twitter.com/centerstreet

First Edition: June 2016

Center Street is a division of Hachette Book Group, Inc. The Center Street name and logo are trademarks of Hachette Book Group, Inc.

The publisher is not responsible for websites (or their content) that are not owned by the publisher.

The Hachette Speakers Bureau provides a wide range of authors for speaking events. To find out more, go to www.HachetteSpeakersBureau.com or call (866) 376-6591.

Print book interior design by Timothy Shaner, NightandDayDesign.biz

Library of Congress Cataloging-in-Publication Data has been applied for.

ISBNs: 978-1-4555-3991-8 (hardcover), 978-1-4555-3990-1 (ebook)

Printed in the United States of America

RRD-C

10 9 8 7 6 5 4 3 2 1

CONTENTS

PREFACE

My first year in Congress has been tough, but although I came into office as an outsider, I was never really fighting alone. I was just following in the tradition of many people fighting for limited government, free markets, and Judeo-Christian ethics who came before me, and this book is the story of that tradition.

It is also the story of applying the principles of that tradition to a congressional campaign that led to my election and shook the Washington establishment. I'm grateful to all the people who helped out on that campaign and to my family—my wife, Laura, and children, Jonathan and Sophia—for sticking by me through all the hard work. I think they were even having fun, at least sometimes. I'm also thankful to Todd Seavey, Kate Hartson, Jennifer Cohen, and the others who helped make possible the book you're reading now, so that I can try to put the whole campaign into perspective and explain what I hope to accomplish in Washington now that I'm there.

I want to thank all the people of Virginia's Seventh District, without whom I wouldn't be there. They gave me the opportunity to serve our country. My volunteers and staff did a fantastic job working with this rookie and putting us into a position to make a new voice heard in our national conversation—maybe begin to turn the ship of state around on some of the issues described in this book.

This is a quick overview of a very long-term struggle, so bear with me if some of the details are glossed over quickly or I've misquoted a medieval sage somewhere along the line. If the sense of the deeper Western culture I'm defending comes through, that is the important thing. I'm not attempting to solve all the world's problems in this volume but instead to take twenty years worth of lecture notes, stump speeches, campaign documents, press clippings, blog citations, policy briefs, economic reports, and the wisdom of the ages and show how all of these ideas can fit together in a systematic whole.

I have long admired efforts to fit the disjointed parts of our philosophical inheritance into a larger whole, to make some sense of how we got to this strange point. I was a liberal arts professor—not the same thing as a "liberal professor," let me stress—for twenty years, and I went to seminary before teaching economics. I love economics, but in that field you sometimes find yourself longing for the ability to step back and contemplate the whole universe that comes more naturally to theologians. Economics these days rarely involves stepping back, looking at the big picture, and asking if we've gotten the fundamentals wrong. The most respected, advanced thinkers in economics are usually brilliant people but are focused on very detailed, technical questions. The systematic part has been left behind. But we need it badly right now.

That is why the classics—of literature, philosophy, religion, and economics—are so valuable. Most philosophers of note throughout our history were system builders. The constitutional regime crafted by the United States' Founders was the icing on the cake of a unique blend of Western civilization ingredients. I believe God had a hand in that process, too, putting some very talented men in place here at just the right time. Their wisdom has left us with the tools to survive difficult times and political confusion, to move forward and fix the flaws in our republic. This book is an attempt to show that we depart from their example—abandon the tools they left us—at our peril. We can return to a systematic way of thinking in which they partook so that our politics, economy, civil society, academics, businesses, military, teachers, and public servants all work in an environment of freedom and optimism again.

I hope we've dotted all the *i*'s and crossed all the *t*'s in this book, but we put it together in an impressionistic fashion in a few short months, so if not every great author is quoted perfectly, we apologize in advance. But we also recall that the classics did not have too many footnotes. They drew upon common knowledge. The great ideas did not belong solely to any particular individual, but the greats still cited one another. They were aware of most of the Canon in those days, not squirreled away in their own niches of technical expertise—and they knew that no one in particular was the Oracle. They assumed that the greatest insights of all likely came from God and from the tradition itself, made up of the great minds that preceded them. That is the attitude I hope to embody.

This is not an excuse for sloppiness, as our goal is to be particularly mindful of giving credit where it's due, just an anticipation of reality, since we live in the age of "gotcha" politics where every sentence can be scoured for the slightest departure from political correctness or the latest revisionist research. My hope is just that you will come away sharing, even if only for the duration of this book, the big picture.

The reader will note, I also hope, that not a sentence in this book is intended to slight any particular person and that I write with the golden rule in mind. Just as I would expect to have people challenge my ideas boldly and firmly, I will do the same. That is what we are called to do in the realm of ideas, and I still believe we can do that, and learn from our contemporaries as well our forebears, without any of us hating each other because of it. Love is part of the solution to our political problems.

INTRODUCTION

I hope voters will conclude that I was motivated by more than a desire for power or fame when I ran for office. Those forces explain a good deal of what goes on in Washington, DC, but when I ran for Congress, what excited me were battles much bigger than one election cycle, the political establishment I faced, and maybe even the gigantic federal debt so many of my constituents justifiably worry about.

This book explains those larger, longer-term battles. The campaign I fought in 2014 was just the latter-day manifestation of an effort, now centuries old, to fuse individual liberty, market economics, the firm foundation of Judeo-Christian ethics, and the rule of law and constitutional government that renders those other goals and institutions possible.

I began my run for office out of the simple recognition that the establishment and oversized federal government are out of touch with the desires of voters and more responsive legislators are needed immediately. There's nothing like being a member of Congress to make you appreciate what a gargantuan task it is to change things there. It wasn't supposed to work this way when the United States was founded as a commercial society with oversight by a carefully crafted *limited* government with enumerated powers.

As I go on to explain, though, this seemingly miraculous formula for a flourishing society didn't arise *ex nihilo*.

Many Americans fail to appreciate it these days, but we are the product of a more than two-thousand-year tradition that has gradually figured out how to protect and celebrate the individual and unleash the creative powers of capitalism. That tradition wasn't always perfect. We had to learn some terrible, harsh lessons, including seeing the French Revolution turn into butchery and tyranny in the late eighteenth century at almost the same time that ours was ushering in liberty and wealth creation the likes of which the common citizen had never before known.

To understand the roots of the Western tradition, we need to look back at its very start, to the philosophy of ancient Athens and the morals of Jerusalem. We will find that both shaped the Roman and post-Roman world, and without Christianity, Rome might well have remained a coldly authoritarian empire. Rome had law but lacked, in a word, love.

The value placed upon every individual soul in Christianity is an ethos that can hold together a far-flung commercial society, not a formula for self-absorption. There are times when collective defense is necessary against external foes or unregulated immigration, but the belief that each person matters is the best, simplest justification for letting everyone live freely. That's not just moral relativism talking, either. As I will recount, Saint Augustine recognized that each soul struggles with earthly temptation, aided by the hope for something above this material plane.[1] It doesn't mean we leave each person unguided by the wisdom of past ages and moral traditions.

Thank goodness the hippie mantra "If it feels good, do it" was not the logical end point of the Western moral tradition.

However, there was a crude approximation of our real moral arc even in the relativism of the 1960s and the postmodernism of the present-day college campus. Individualism guided by moral traditions, property rights, and the rule of law can bring a more lasting, sustainable happiness than the chaos of relativism ever could.

I'll also show how the Western tradition in recent centuries led to both the triumph of free markets and the terrible intellectual error of socialism. (*Socialism* might be almost too fancy a word for the irresponsible, debt-ridden mess of our twenty-first-century big government.) I will conclude with a sketch of the "ethics of liberty" that can still save us from fiscal ruin and show how I apply those ethics to legislative battles I fight every day that the voters see fit to let me serve them in Congress.

The goal of this book is to keep the big-picture conversation going, not solve every complex issue under the sun. The beauty of the truth in its full complexity may be beyond our perception, but we all sense it calling to us. It is certainly good to put on paper what we can, test our claims in the public arena, and try to deduce which truths work best for real people within history. You will see that I just barely wade into some of the deep, deep philosophical questions in the Western tradition. I am cautious on purpose. I want the next generation to take up the quest and push us all to do even better.

In this life I have been blessed to teach students for more than twenty years. The biggest blessing is when my former students tell me that I made a difference in their lives. I compelled them to think. (I would not allow them to wear flip-flops to class, either.) So in this spirit, let's take a look at a historic election and the ideas and people that made it happen.

chapter one

VICTORY, OR AT LEAST A START

My political candidacy was never merely an antiestablishment rebellion, though it was that, too.

My unexpected victory in the 2014 Republican primary for US Representative for Virginia's Seventh District shocked the press and the political establishment. I defeated then–House Majority Leader Eric Cantor, who had been talked about as a possible successor to Ohio's John Boehner as Speaker of the House. We now know that Boehner has acknowledged that Cantor was in line to be Speaker.[1] As the press made clear after the victory, no one in US history had ever defeated a sitting majority leader.[2] In truth, if I had completely thought through all the implications of this victory, I might have had more than second thoughts, but it all worked out, and there is something to the saying "Sufficient unto the day are the evils thereof."

The Associated Press called the victory "stunning."[3] The *Washington Post*'s Chris Cillizza tweeted, "This Cantor loss is *seismically* large. Can't remember when I have been so surprised."[4] "Holy crap,"

1

said BuzzFeed and many others.[5] The Hill reported that "being Cantored" became a term used on Capitol Hill by members and staffers fearful of primary defeats by more conservative candidates.[6]

The Need for a Political Change

A few months earlier, when I was deciding whether to run, I had been reading books that included *Freakonomics* by Steven D. Levitt and Stephen J. Dubner and *David and Goliath* by Malcolm Gladwell, both reminders that old, predictable patterns in politics and economics don't always hold. In my stump speeches, I told people that in many ways Gladwell's book illustrated that true power is not always what it appears to be. Some people who appear to have tremendous strength in one area have weaknesses in other areas. In politics, I believe that true power derives from the people, and if you really believe that, other typical power sources such as campaign funding and negative advertising may not mean as much. At least, that was my bet. For most of the campaign, I put a sign on the door of my study that read, "The things which are impossible with men are possible with God" (Luke 18:27). Boy, did I see that play out on almost a daily basis. Everyone said I was crazy, it couldn't be done, and there was no possible way on earth I could win.

The comedian Stephen Colbert poked fun at my giving thanks to God for my victory, saying sarcastically, "Yes, Brat's victory was a miracle from God."[7] As usual, the media like to read arrogance into expressions of faith, but they're really statements of humility and frank amazement.

People attempted to dissect my statement and give an account of how the miracle could have happened. You can tell some convincing stories, but in the end it was still a miracle. No one quite understood where it came from. In this book I'll try to explain what led up to it all, but it's not a story that starts a few months before the primary election day. It starts more than two thousand years earlier.

In the afternoons, after half a day of working on the campaign, I would usually take a short break to reflect. I would look up into the sky and say something like a little prayer: "This burden's way too big for me to handle. I need some help. Lighten my load." Over the weeks that ensued, the strength I needed seemed to come in a variety of forms while the political forces arrayed against me showed their moral weaknesses. I always remembered God telling others to stand back and watch the mighty arm of God. And then friends from across the district told me they were praying. Many, many prayed. I had never known that this spiritual force existed in such a powerful way. But it was not just ethereal. It took shape in the politics of Virginia.

For instance, I benefited from growing awareness among Virginia voters about an underhanded technical procedure called "slating" that allowed the state political machine to stop conservative voters from choosing their own district and regional party leaders across Virginia.[8] We were told that in one instance of slating about 900 people showed up in Virginia Beach to a meeting they considered to be part of the democratic process only, but the party higher-ups sent about 870 folks home. It's a technical rule meant to allow Republicans to send interloper Democrats packing, but no one ever imagined that Republicans would send fellow Republicans home.[9] This type of machine politics is one of the main reasons I ran. Powerful elites want to ensure control of business and government contracts, and the surest way to do that is to get their own yes-men into the inner circles of government.

Despite the outrage over slating in Virginia Beach, the machine pressed on, eventually landing in Henrico County. Angry at the political process and how it was manipulated, the grass roots came out in full force, their patriotic fervor energizing the entire region to show up and block the plans to slate candidates in my own county. Due to those citizens' hard work, slating did not occur in my county, Eric Cantor's home county, even though the machine had succeeded in using the tactic elsewhere around the state.[10]

A few weeks before my win on June 10, there was a Seventh District committee meeting to determine the chairman for the district. The grass roots ran its candidate against Eric Cantor's point man. The room was packed with hundreds of people, which rarely occurs. It showed the fever pitch of the passion for restoring good government in our area. Yet although I was running for office, this was also the meeting in which I was told I was not allowed to speak and the meeting organizers would not give our side a copy of the rules, which they manipulated at every step. Shortly after the meeting began, they invited the Senate candidates to speak but then quickly moved on to the next item on the agenda. Toward the end of the meeting, someone finally tracked down a copy of the rules stating that each candidate was permitted to speak for five minutes.[11]

During Eric Cantor's speech, the crowd booed, which was a bit embarrassing for our side. The national press left out the entire context of the statewide manipulation of rules and the attempt to steal elections from the American people, not just from me.[12] Booing may not be polite, but in my view it was done only in response to those major grievances. In fact, the booing was loudest when Cantor repeated his negative claims, such as calling me a "liberal professor." Ironically, though the press was critical of the booing directed at Cantor, it somehow failed to notice that the very negative five-million-dollar ad campaign[13] he directed against me featured a cartoon of a crowd booing me.

The establishment gets away with all sorts of things outsiders do not.

The Political Elite

This is just one of the instances in our story when the usual right/left lines matter less than the division between the establishment and the rest of us.

If you study the budget process in the US Congress, you will find that the left and the right are not represented much in any final deal. Instead, the true action is in the middle. That is where you will find the money. The leadership on both sides arrange for the old Christmas budget surprise. It hijacks the budget out of committee and throws in all the toys it wants, and a $4 trillion budget emerges that blows the caps, increases the deficit by half a trillion dollars, and supports every special interest known to man. The votes lately have been very bipartisan. The press never makes this clear because that story is not so dramatic. It is just true.

The political establishment in both parties has also failed to address voters' worries about illegal immigration, the refugee crisis, and the open southern border. The linkage between these issues and national security/terrorism is by far the number one issue in the presidential election this year as well. The candidates who are listening to "We the People" are winning in the polls. I listened two years back, and immigration was already resonating then. The working person is not happy with the lower wages and constant pressure created by elites' importing more cheap labor from abroad. That wasn't the sole reason for my victory, but the immigration issue is emblematic of the divide between establishment and populace. I think most folks are with me in my position against illegal immigration. Conservative media personalities, including Laura Ingraham, Mark Levin, and regional radio hosts, weighed in to support me in part because of that issue. The Chamber of Commerce and some of the corporate heavy-weights want cheap labor, but they don't want to pay the full cost of inviting millions of newcomers into our country. It's pretty simple: if you have a person who immigrates and makes $20,000 a year and pays very little in taxes but has two kids in the public schools, the cost to the taxpayer is $26,000. Business gets cheap labor, and the rest of us get that $26,000 bill.

Try running that by the voters someday and see how they react. Teaching people about this issue resonated with residents in the Seventh District of Virginia and resulted in a new political aware-ness that eventually became one of the leading political issues in the presidential campaigns of 2016. There are good reasons voters in both parties felt they needed to turn to "outsider" candidates: the insiders weren't listening.

After I won my election and news stories came out about it, we learned there were a lot of other candidates who had tried to run on similar ideas but had not been met with the same success. The force stopping them was one of the main reasons I ran for office: the major corruption at all levels of government. Major political machines keep people from getting involved even in their county breakfast meetings. You may want to run for school board, but if you're not the right well-connected person, you are told you can't run. Then if you decide to run for state delegate or state senate or higher office, it is hard to get equipped. It becomes even more of a miracle story selecting these folks than getting me elected, though they may be highly qualified, patriotic Americans.

At this point, I want to thank all the folks in the grass roots of Virginia who aided our great win. Many, many wonderful people have spent years sacrificing for such a win. Some gave up wealth, time, and family; others ran for office themselves but did not get the win. But they all laid the foundation for change in Virginia, and many of our ideas are now spreading across the nation at the highest levels. This book is dedicated to the volunteers who worked for me but really worked for the greatest political experiment on earth, the United States of America. Without them, my own piece would count for little. In fact, I had run earlier and smacked into a brick wall.

I ran for office four years prior to winning my seat, so I was not a complete novice. Unfortunately, that race, for the House of Delegates in Virginia, was manipulated in every way possible. I saw there was no way for me to go through the regular political process in my region and expect any kind of fair outcome. I noticed Washington setting the tone for machine politics and cronyism at the state and local levels, so the problem at the top had to be solved. I started thinking about challenging Eric Cantor because his team was orchestrating much of the political nonsense in my region.

The political process is manipulated to achieve certain ends for favored people, the special interests. Instead of focusing on the interests of the American people and the needs of his Seventh District constituents, I think Cantor had grown detached. My campaign highlighted those differences by focusing on the Republican Creed and noting that there is no problem with it; the problem is that the political machine and the political elites don't follow any part of it.

Everyone always liked good old Dave, as long as I was teaching their kids and sticking to economics and ethics. But when I actually started to run on a platform of free markets and holding others accountable in public, I quickly learned that everyone is in favor of free markets in general but not for his own business.

"Are you nuts, Dave? Do you know what would happen to our firm if we lost the special protections we have and the subsidies we get from the taxpayer?"

"Dave, you understand, don't you? I have to do what's right for my firm. In fact, that is the ethical thing to do. I have a fiduciary responsibility to fleece the taxpayer to protect my shareholder."

If this pattern becomes the rule instead of the corrupt exception, our country is gone. Really.

I had never been interested in political power for its own sake. I would have been very happy doing economics at the state level or helping federal candidates behind the scenes because I felt it was my duty to educate people about some of the problems we face. I ran for office only when I saw the corruption of the political machines and felt something had to be done about it.

My decision to run for office later in life was not only practical but tied to deeper political wisdom. Plato, in *The Republic*, advised that one should enter politics at the age of fifty, likely close to the average age of death in 400 BC. Reason should rule, and younger folks are oftentimes tempted by the passions and what Plato called the "appetites." He and Saint Augustine both felt that going into politics is a serious undertaking, which should take place after the appetites of wine, women, and song have faded. Augustine laid out the normal progression from concern with appearances to money to power to politics and ultimately, hopefully, to faith in God. Aristotle would similarly counsel that the practical wisdom and prudence required for proper politics must come partly from experience. It is by no means a realm for book smarts. A life well lived requires discipline, training, and virtue in pursuit of excellence. True happiness results only if this path is followed. The Catholic vision articulated by Saint Thomas Aquinas more than a thousand years later would add the Christian virtues of faith, hope, and love.

A Grassroots Response

God works in mysterious ways, but in most cases God works through people. I could not have won without the support of hundreds and perhaps thousands of people toiling across all nine counties of my district (Culpeper, Orange, Spotsylvania, Louisa, Goochland, Chesterfield, Hanover, Henrico, and New Kent) and the city of Richmond. Many people made signs. Others spread the word through their organizations and e-mail lists. Some called in other regions of the state to knock on doors. I had superheroes in each county who knocked on thousands of doors for me. Thousands. (I found most of this out after our big win.)

I'm also grateful that among those supporters were my wife, Laura, my son, Jonathan (who said the night of my victory that he always thought I'd win—thanks, son), and my daughter, Sophia. My wife deserves the most credit of all. It is one thing for folks to take cheap shots at me. Within a day they fade away. But to have someone take a cheap shot at your spouse is even worse. Naturally, Laura went out of her way to make sure I was portrayed in a fair way. When folks used foul language anywhere near my campaign, she stepped in and clarified that I do not condone hate or negative campaigning. I had always advised my staff that every word we put down on paper and every word from every consultant or writer or blogger should convey who I am: a seminary graduate with a PhD in economics and someone who tries to love everyone I meet. Any messaging should follow those rules.

Others who helped me, though, died long before I arrived on the scene. Our region of the state was home to American Revolution leaders Patrick Henry, Thomas Jefferson, and James Madison, among others. I'd like to think that the supporters of my campaign were carrying on those revolutionaries' work.

If you want a down-to-earth view of the miracle that was that congressional campaign, look at the way the people of the Seventh District responded to the campaign. In many ways they were ahead of the rest of the country, the first wave of a rediscovery of our founding principles: the importance of the Constitution and equal treatment under the law for all people (not just the special people), as well as the necessity for fiscal restraint and the free-market system.

I ran on these principles, and the people gave me tremendous support. Imagining 100 million American households much like our own suffering from bad policies in Washington should be enough to motivate anyone to fight the establishment, but this wasn't just an angry, antiestablishment campaign.

The press openly mocked my twenty-minute economic talks because I wasn't reciting a typical stump speech. But the people liked them. And the people are all that matters. So the energy level in the district was incredible, and some of the pros told me that whoever has energy on his side will end up winning. During my first year in office it was energizing making frequent visits across my district, touring neighborhoods, and getting to know as many voters as possible—something too few politicians get a chance to do once they're in DC, which may be part of the problem.

Having a government by the people and for the people means that legislators should never get too accustomed to being apart from the people they were elected to represent. I pledged to term limit myself to twelve years in the Congress. Term limits are needed to break up special interest money, engrained power structures, and crony relationships that result in doling out our $4 trillion budget. Some politicians care only about climbing the ladder so they can chair an important committee. Vote yes on everything your leadership wants, and you play a game that will bankrupt the country. This shows the importance of serving for a limited time and returning to your community. The Founding Fathers could not have imagined the concept of career politicians. This stance and my willingness to push and vote for term limits separates me from many politicians, who will not take that pledge or who go back on it if they do. I always said the race was not about me, and I actually mean that the people won the race. Many people laid the foundation years before me: activists, bloggers, grassroots leaders, politicians who won or even lost races but who supported ideas, social connections, databases, and energy that would help push constitutional and free-market thought in later years.

Finally, I tried to run a positive campaign, even when the same thing could not be said about my primary opponent: The Cantor campaign spent about $5 million running false negative ads against me, implying that I was going to push Grandma off the cliff and I was a liberal college professor. (The *Washington Post* and others called me a right-wing candidate, so I guess someone must have had it wrong.) Many of my voters received a flyer in the mail every day saying such things, but they looked into it and found that Cantor's campaign was making inaccurate claims, to put it mildly. In the Seventh District, the truth is at a premium, and miraculously, that $5 million pitted against my $200,000 ended up convincing people that I was facing an arrogant machine. My opponents thought they could buy the election by simply running ads filled with patent falsehoods. Thank goodness that was not the case.

My opponent had the endorsement of just about every politician in the entire region, and I still won the race—so I guess I can give hope to other Davids going through David-and-Goliath stories. I didn't have any endorsements, and I didn't have any outside money or big outside groups supporting me. (To give you some idea of how little money we had toward the end of the campaign, we had only a thousand dollars to purchase yard signs, so my loyal constituents took the existing signs and moved them from property to property every few days to maximize my name ID and remind people to vote on June 10.) I was told that the odds of electing me were extremely low.

But I had something better. I had friends like Major, who put signs in the back of his pickup and drove around telling friends and neighbors about an economics professor who was speaking the truth. I had many, many other friends whom I cannot name here, but my new chief and campaign manager has always shouldered more than his share. I'm so grateful to all those volunteers, across the region and even across the country, and to my campaign staff, not to mention every last donor who pitched in twenty dollars. Every little bit made a difference. To all those people, I can only say I am humbled by you, my true friends. God bless.

Maybe the local spirits of Patrick Henry and James Madison— or the patriotic impulse in their DNA—helped to motivate this miracle as well.

Thrust into the Spotlight

On June 10, 2014, the night we won the primary, of course we had national TV coverage. For the next two days I was basically in a bunker fielding phone calls. I'm not kidding when I say

I received calls from numerous foreign countries. I specifically remember China, Saudi Arabia, and Japan. People arrived from all over the state, not just the region, to figure out how it could have happened. Local and national news crews camped out in the cul-de-sac in front of our driveway. My kids couldn't go outside.

One morning the press approached me as I walked out of the house. I said, "I'm going to get a haircut. I'm not ready to talk." The press reported the news as: "Dave Brat says he's not prepared to handle questions."

So that was the beginning of my experience with the press while we were trying to staff up for bigger and better things.

A Government Out of Touch

Through all of it, I wasn't campaigning against only one member of Congress, and I don't mean to pick on him in particular. He's one of many members who have repeatedly voted to raise the debt ceiling, bail out large corporations, support an endless stream of massive pork-laden spending bills that increase the national debt, and cheerlead for amnesty for illegal immigration. Cantor pushed that last goal a bit farther than most, though, even delivering a speech billed as a new agenda for the Republican Party in which he declared that citizenship for illegals was required by "the great founding principles of our country."

Cantor took a leading role in crafting the House leadership's amnesty plan, which, according to a report in the *New York Times*, would provide potentially 6.5 million illegal immigrants with citizenship and bring in more guest workers for corporations looking to lay off Americans.[14] The only reason Cantor's amnesty plan isn't law today is that members saw the American people rise up and say, "No!" In fact, an October 20, 2015, PBS documentary chronicled the "Immigration Battle" turnaround, and it dramatically shows that the key date was June 10, 2014, the day of our stunning victory. The Democrats were dejected and also made it clear that Cantor's losing was the ending point for their efforts on amnesty. My values do not usually allow for spiking the ball in the end zone, but in this case, it becomes very frustrating when some people continue to say that we have not accomplished anything. What they mean is that we have not pushed for more endless federal government programs. In fact, the people of the Seventh District brought an end to the "Gang of Eight" immigration bill and to amnesty legislation in general. That is a huge accomplishment. It helps our workers, it has made the nation safer, and it has brought a new awareness to all the related issues in the presidential election this year.

The immigration issue is important to average voters not just because of the harm mass immigration might do to them but because it underscores the fact that Congress doesn't represent everyone but instead large corporations seeking a never-ending supply of cheap foreign labor regardless of the effects on US workers. As summarized by Charles Blow in the *New York Times*, the nonpartisan Pew Research Center wrote in a new report: "In 1990, the U.S. had 19.8 million immigrants. That number rose to a record 40.7 million immigrants in 2012, among them 11.7 million unauthorized immigrants. Over this period, the number of immigrants in the U.S. increased more than five times as much as the U.S.-born population."[15] This unprecedented flow of low-wage workers has pulled down wages for everyone, including recent legal immigrants.

And without getting too far into the weeds, if the average illegal immigrant makes about $20,000 a year, maybe pays a bit of that in taxes, and has two kids in public schools, who pays the $26,000 a year for that education? And who pays for the emergency room and other programs? So the big firms get cheap labor, and the people foot the bill for all the costs. Same logic with Obamacare in general: firms get more clients, and the people pick up the tab. Getting the logic here? Judging by the presidential polls at the time of this writing, I would say you are!

Maybe I'm naive, but I'm more interested in getting continuous feedback from my Seventh District constituents than in pleasing big corporations and government agencies. The message from those constituents seems to be: Dave is actually doing what he promised he would do; he ran on principles; he's voting on those principles; he listens to us; his voting card is not for sale; and we're proud that he is our congressman. That gives me joy beyond expression. I hope we'd make Patrick Henry, James Madison, and other freedom-fighting forebears proud, too, because there's no reason we have to surrender and become a nation of bureaucracies and dying hope.

Among those refusing to surrender are the activists, volunteers, and staffers who worked so diligently on my insurgent campaign. They came to us from the Tea Party, the Republican Party, the Libertarian Party, and the Democratic Party, along with many independents. We had the gun guys, the church friends, the home school friends, and the many freedom groups that organize nationally and meet locally. Their enthusiasm helped persuade the citizens of the Commonwealth of Virginia to entrust me with a great honor by sending me to Congress. In return I'm going to fight to get the country moving in the right direction again.

Considering Washington's out-of-control spending, the poor employment outlook, and the failing economy, it's easy to be pessimistic about our nation's future. But working on my congressional campaign—and then with the small but effective House Freedom Caucus in Congress—gave me hope. We've shown the country that citizens can still make their voices heard and reclaim a government of the people, by the people, and for the people. Principles and good ideas can still prevail in a system all too often dominated by cynicism, special-interest money, and cronyism. I vowed to work every day to restore trust in American institutions, values, and principles. In Washington, I'll work with anyone else who is committed to principled solutions and good-faith efforts to solve our nation's challenges.

In just one year, the House Freedom Caucus had a major impact on leadership, resulting in changes at the top, and returned the House to regular order in its operations. This means the budget can no longer be hijacked by leadership. It stays in the budget committee, on which I sit. It then moves to twelve appropriations bills, and that is the end. No more smoke-filled rooms for the special interests. This is a huge accomplishment and will result in billions of dollars in savings this year alone and hopefully in trillions as we tackle the mandatory programs in the years to come. The mandatory issue is now at the $100 trillion unfunded mark and will use up all federal revenues in eleven years—with not a dime left for our national defense, education, or transportation; see the CBO graph "Autopilot Spending Exceeds All Revenue by 2027" near the end of this chapter[16] and share it with others. So we still have significant lifting to do, but this is an important start.

I'll continue to focus on the same issues I campaigned on: jump-starting our economy, securing our border, reducing the overwhelming tax burden on our families and businesses, protecting retirement programs for our seniors, and replacing Obamacare with reforms that actually lower costs. I've tried to focus on the large issues facing our nation more than the partisan barbs back and forth. My election helped start a national conversation on solving serious prob-

lems with the political establishment, and—as Ronald Reagan said—
we tried to appeal to people's best hopes and not their worst fears.
I hope that going forward, the media can partner with us to focus
more on critical issues rather than on personalities. I think the people are better served that way, and, as in the classroom, people will
rise to meet the challenge if you present them with substantial ideas.

As an educator for more than twenty years and Congress's only
economist, I shared regularly with the citizens of the Seventh District how proposed taxes, regulations, and spending at the federal
level affect their lives, liberty, and wallets. I wanted to provide that
information directly, not through any filters, explaining why our
conservative, free-market principles are what will bring our country back and why bigger government has been a problem rather than
a solution. Once a month I meet with constituents from nine counties and the city of Richmond in the Seventh District, urging them
to hold me accountable. It's not easy, but that was my pledge and I
have kept my word. My seat belongs to the people, not to the system
in Washington. Indeed, the system itself must be held accountable.
That way, I hope, we can still restore America's greatness and ensure
that the American dream of liberty, security, and economic opportunity remains alive for future generations.

The Media Can Also Be Out of Touch

The mission to restore America's greatness and ensure the
American dream seems clear to me, but for some reason the
press has a hard time reporting on these issues without making it
sound as if anyone who sticks up for American workers must be
motivated by intolerance.

One night in the House, well after midnight, I listened to my
colleagues defending a bill that would grant citizenship to anyone

willing to serve in the military. Some members pleaded the case that it's almost certain that if people want to join the military of the United States of America, they must be good people and we should welcome them with open arms. I stood up and said, "I don't think that's necessarily the case. I think ISIS also would love to be in our military. Isn't that true?" The next day I woke up, got my cup of coffee, read the news, and soon found the *Huffington Post* and a few liberal groups saying that Dave Brat calls little children and dreamers ISIS terrorists.

Of course I was horrified. I had spent years working at the World Bank on behalf of little children around the world. But I let it go. Within a couple of days, the *Huffington Post* story showed up in my local paper in the news, not the opinion section. I called the *Richmond Times-Dispatch* and told them it was all false, and within the next day or so, there were two or three more articles bombarding me on that issue because I guess that's how you win in politics on the left. In the end I wrote a piece that gave the context, and my voters found out the truth. Yet newspapers continue their sloppy reporting without much consequence, and something needs to change. Ironically, momentum has built for candidates like me who tell the truth early on. By contrast, newspapers look terrible, since they have undermined their most vital role in society: conveying the truth.

Once, the *Washington Post* asked to shadow me for a full day in my office and in committee. That is somewhat analogous to being called by the head of the Mafia and told it has a deal that's too good for you to pass up. If you want to participate, you can be sure the *Washington Post* will not do a love story on conservatives, but if you refuse it will come out sounding even worse. I was concerned but agreed to do the story, and the reporter and I actually enjoyed the day on the Hill together. I knew they were kind of digging around, and other reporters looked over my office as well, taking photos of my picture of Jesus walking on stormy water, which they'd like to read into, though for me it's mainly a reminder of how difficult it is for virtue to survive in Washington and how much you need calm and an inner peace when things get tough.

One reporter noticed the coasters on the table that said "Louisa loves you." The reporter asked who Louisa is, and I said that was one of the counties I represent, and most people get a kick out of that story, especially my friends in Louisa. Then they took about a thousand pictures of me, though usually no matter how much you smile, the picture turns out less than flattering. (In Congress, we always tease each other about who has the worst pictures.)

Then my good friend Congressman Tom Massie added to the drama of the day. I'd told him the *Post* was coming, so he followed me down the stairs in the Cannon House Office Building and at the top of his lungs yelled, "Go get 'em, Dragon Slayer!"

Finally, the story came out, and it was the normal hit piece, all right, and of course I was unable to convey my fundamental positions and was upset that even reporters are not that interested in covering the points I emphasize over and over again: the $19 trillion in debt we've racked up and our $100 trillion in unfunded liabilities—the most important topics for the welfare of our country and our children. So although the issues got no traction, you bet they put the Massie humor in the first paragraph. Members of the press love a clash of personalities—and stories of clashes between leadership and the base—but they ignore the fundamental issues that cause those tensions.

At least the *Post* admits it sometimes does "personality" pieces. It's more disturbing when PolitiFact repeatedly calls you, believing various charges made by your better-established political opponents, and then if you show your opponents were bluffing, it drops the story instead of turning the tables on the liars. The media are not as objective as they pretend to be, and that makes it easier for politicians to get away with deceptions. By the way, who owns and runs PolitiFact? The liberal *Tampa Bay Times*. Always follow the money. No surprises on the bias when you do. It will not come as a shock to you that after each and every major conservative accomplishment, I was hit with a PolitiFact. It's not worth it to correct all its mistakes in this book, but if you study journalism ethics I will be happy to provide you with extended endnotes for your research.

One of my experiences talking to TV host Chuck Todd sums up the dangers of dealing with the press rather well. He gave me about twenty minutes to go on about how minimum-wage laws work, why they're actually a bad idea, and how the wage graph is basically our national productivity graph, a pattern you cannot really cheat over the long run. All that was for naught, since in the edited show only a thirty-second clip was aired, as if that were all I knew on the topic, and Todd attacked me for failing to answer his questions. That's pretty typical.

It's not just DC media, either. I had hoped the *Richmond Times-Dispatch*—my local paper—might be fair to me since officially it shares my Judeo-Christian outlook and even a fondness for the philosopher Immanuel Kant. But when I asked them whether they thought an ad my opponent Cantor was running was true, they got upset, told me Cantor is their friend, and left out the many conflicts of interest they had in their reporting. There was no rational give-and-take. They own the ink. And I guess sometimes that is the last word.

To be fair, in DC the press has begun to give me a bit of a break lately. In early 2016, my work on the budget committee was highlighted favorably in Politico, The Hill, and *Roll Call*. A few of the facts manage to break through. However, while I keep my own side honest as best I can, it is amazing how the press never puts similar pressure on the Democrats. The Democrats rarely create any budget, never produce a balanced budget, have no plans to save the mandatory programs and keep the next generation in the game. None. The press knows all this is true. It pushes details about balance on our side during negotiations but won't even broach the issue of balance on the other side. The press doesn't say, "Hey, Nancy Pelosi, is it true that you have no budget plans whatsoever? . . . Oh, you do have one? Can you shoot the white paper over this afternoon? . . . Oh, the e-mail is down?" On it goes.

The Biggest Issue: A Very Big Debt

If the most important issues were guaranteed ratings, we would be hearing about topics such as immigration pros and cons, national security, the refugee crisis in the Middle East and Latin America, Russia's land grabs, Chinese provocations, the terrible nuclear antimonitoring agreement with Iran—including the Corker-Cardin bill, which I voted against because it wasn't even enforceable (and was almost mockingly followed by Iran purchasing Airbus planes and boosting its missile production capacity)—and expansion of the hell on earth that is the ISIS terrorist pseudostate in Syria and Iraq. Do we even have a strategy in Syria?

Looming over everything is our massive debt, which we rarely admit in our lofty speeches and which seriously hampers our ability to do anything bold or constructive around the world, militarily or otherwise. At the end of his term, the former chairman of the Joint Chiefs of Staff declared that the greatest military threat to this nation is the national debt. He gets it. This is the nation that set up the Bretton Woods global monetary system and the liberal political order of the mid–twentieth century, promulgated the very idea of human rights, and intervened militarily when necessary to defend that humane and prosperous system—with almost no one else helping out. Relative to the rest of the world, we're not rich enough to get away with that anymore.

But we could be. And the key is rediscovering our faith in individual liberty instead of badly managed, collectivist government solutions.

The graph below, "Leaving a Legacy of Debt to Our Kids," (which reflects what were the "most recent" CBO numbers back in January 2016) is a good indicator of the magnitude of our economic problem. We've just crossed the $19 trillion mark for federal debt, a crushing load that is not only an economic problem but an ethical one, and it now looks likely to get much worse.

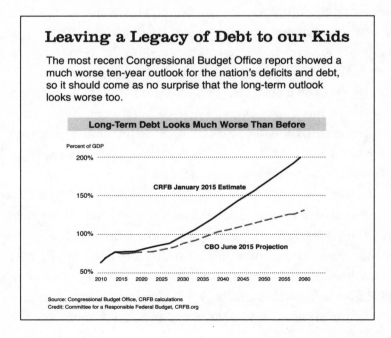

Leaving a Legacy of Debt to our Kids

The most recent Congressional Budget Office report showed a much worse ten-year outlook for the nation's deficits and debt, so it should come as no surprise that the long-term outlook looks worse too.

Long-Term Debt Looks Much Worse Than Before

Percent of GDP

CRFB January 2015 Estimate

CBO June 2015 Projection

Source: Congressional Budget Office, CRFB calculations
Credit: Committee for a Responsible Federal Budget, CRFB.org

This is one of the major issues that I ran on, the other being unfunded liabilities, future mandatory federal government payments of about $100 trillion dollars. But let me explain what that means in the context of this year's budget. This year alone we are adding $500 billion to the debt and blowing the budget caps to do so. The Congressional Budget Office expects our deficits to climb to $1 trillion *per year* by 2026, and the total debt will zoom from $19 trillion to $30 trillion in the next decade. See "Autopilot Spending Exceeds All Revenue by 2027" below.

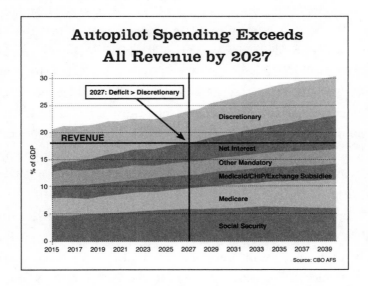

In eleven years, in 2027 on the graph above, *all* federal revenues will go to entitlement and mandatory programs. After that, we will have $100 trillion in unfunded liabilities. That's not the total cost of the programs—that is just *the part we cannot afford*, the scheduled spending beyond revenues, that which we cannot pay but have promised by law to seniors and those with health concerns. Under current law, the reality is that all federal revenues go to these programs without one dollar left in the budget for the military, education, transportation, or any other program. This is not an argument for getting rid of Social Security or Medicare; it is an argument for reforming our whole system before it collapses and we are unable to meet any of our promises to the kids who will not get any benefits.

Right now, discretionary spending (the piece at the top of the graph) is one-third of the budget, and mandatory entitlement spending (all the shades beneath discretionary)—sometimes also called autopilot spending—is currently two-thirds. For instance, if I am on the Budget Committee in Congress, our committee can address only the discretionary part of the budget. The rest is set by law and can be changed only by putting a bill through the House and the Senate and then overcoming a veto from the president. So today we on the committee control one-third of the budget, but in eleven years we will have no control over the budget, since the entire budget—all federal revenues—will go only to mandatory spending. We will have no money left for discretionary spending unless we deficit spend the entire discretionary part of the budget.

According to the board of trustees' reports on Social Security[17] and Medicare,[18] both programs will become insolvent by 2034 (just seven years after we hit the point when all federal spending goes to entitlements). The students I talk to every day—seniors in high school and college students who will retire in, say, fifty years—would see dramatic reductions in these programs. Many kids think the programs won't even be in existence by then, so they're already cynical about their futures.

It's obvious that those programs need major reforms if they are going to exist for our children and the next generation, and this is a moral imperative as well as a potential economic disaster.

The problem in Washington, DC, is not that people do not understand this. The real problem, unfortunately, is moral. Solving the moral problem will require tremendous courage and backbone to address these controversial issues. Paul Ryan is talking about a bold new agenda for 2017 to tackle corporate tax reform, Obamacare replacement, and entitlement reform. That is Ryan's expertise, and he has acknowledged that there's basically a tight four-year window to get it right. If we don't win the presidency in 2016, those reforms may well never happen, and we will have to face terrible consequences for our kids. So the time is now. It is critical that we fight for these economic reforms to get this country back on track.

Our staggering debt and slowing economic growth mean that our children graduating from high school and college will already have a hard time. Our economy grew only 0.7 percent in the last quarter of 2015.[19] Our students have to compete against the best in the world and are struggling to find jobs as it is. They will make an entry-level salary, pay a third of that in taxes, and then pay off the federal debt on top of the hardships they encounter. In other words, in terms I might use teaching Economics 101, we've been having a pizza party, spending more than we take in every year, and we are leaving our children the tab. It is completely unethical, and it has to stop.

Of course, the debt load is also a threat to financial markets. Back in 2007–2008, our country was indebted on all fronts, business and government. Greatly multiply the effect of that financial crisis to get an idea of how big the next one may be. China is currently going through a debt crisis of its own, and its economy is suffering a shock. That in turn is delivering a shock to our economy.

On the House Budget Committee, I have been working very hard to turn this debt crisis around. With a promise of regular order—real review of spending legislation by members instead of rubber-stamping leadership's massive bills—there is some hope this year. Maybe the budget will stay in committee and not get hijacked by leadership at the end of the year as it has the past two years. There should be a real budget and then twelve appropriations bills that work their way through all members of Congress. If that happens, there is a chance we can at least begin to turn the ship around.

Right now, interest rates are almost zero due to the Federal Reserve's policy of printing money to sustain our economy, essentially a sugar high that cannot last. And as interest rates go back up to normal—3, 4, or 5 percent—it will dramatically add to the pressure on our budget. We will all be paying interest on the debt instead of investing in our economy. In February 2016, I saw the Fed contemplating negative interest rates. This is happening while we are deficit spending and stimulating the economy by $500 billion this year as well.[20] On top of everything, the Fed contends that the economic fundamentals are solid. Wow. The Fed is basically cheerleading because it does not have any other option. It is out of bullets.

Ethics, Economics, and Politics Are Linked

It is not unduly materialistic or selfish for a Christian to worry about these matters. In fact, it is a moral duty no matter what your tradition.

God does not hate individualism. As a Calvinist in the broader Judeo-Christian tradition (Calvin paid more attention to Jewish scripture than any other major theologian), I can easily say along with my Jewish brothers and sisters that we, too, make a strong claim to our own lives. God gave us our lives and told us to love others as we love ourselves. We do have a right to ourselves. That is what freedom of conscience is all about. God speaks to us "individually." We are morally responsible as individuals. Nations do not love. Individuals can. The protection of the individual is what caused our communities and society to thrive. The Judeo-Christian tradition is the home of individual freedom and human rights. We invented them. We put them into law. We have expanded them and protected them at every opportunity, knowing that human nature is weak. We have the only system that works in the real world.

We also love production. God worked six days and rested on the Sabbath. Hint, hint. Do not steal—that rule presumes private property. Do not covet—that rule presumes a right to hold things that may be coveted. And so on. The Pilgrims started their production system using the communal method, hoping all would chip in, work hard, and share their crops. Total failure. They next doled out private parcels of land, and the owners and workers were able to keep their own production. Total success. It is really that simple. People work harder and smarter when they own the pride and the product of their work.

The Judeo-Christian tradition matters. After all, James Madison, the primary author of our Constitution, was educated by clergy, went to the College of New Jersey (now Princeton University), took Hebrew after graduating just for kicks, and quoted Calvin on human nature in *The Federalist Papers*. This worldview informed the genius of our founding document. The logic worked to produce the greatest nation on earth. The First Amendment, for example, is routinely summarized today as a protection against government interference with speech, but keep in mind the continent of religious warfare and governmental interference with faith that the inhabitants of the new United States had fled. When the First Amendment says, even before mentioning speech, "Congress shall make no law respecting an establishment of religion, or prohibiting the free exercise thereof," it is a historic victory against sometimes violent internal conflict in the Judeo-Christian tradition. Our founding was an important chapter in the history of faith.

It is also interesting that the architecture of Madison's Constitution is similar to the logic of Adam Smith's free-market economics. Both knew that a large number of competing individuals would foster creativity and keep monopolies from gaining power and lording it over the people. Neither would recognize their theory in the world of $4 trillion budgets doled out to special interests, mainly in business. Today, to compete in the market you need a lobbyist instead of a good product at a low price. Madison urged us to create an order with many factions competing against one another. Today, the one faction without a lobbyist is the kids. So they get all the debt. They will pay our tab. The big corporations can make it work in this crony-state nexus, but the small guy cannot. Business creation is not thriving at all, and some of the biggest firms use regulations to keep little guys from entering the market. Small community banks are going out of business one by one. This needs to change.

To add insult to injury, some call this capitalism! No. Using government to get your way and avoid competition is not free market. It is socialism. Many businesses are just fine and dandy with this arrangement, but the country is not.

It need not be only a few isolated philosophers or radicals who believe in freedom. Individual freedom gives rise to the emergent order of the traditions and communities through which we live. Free Americans combine to give fetes, found seminaries, build churches, distribute books, and send missionaries to the antipodes. Hospitals, prisons, and schools are created that way. Finally, if Americans want to proclaim a truth or propagate some feeling by the encouragement of a good example, they form an association. In every case, at the head of any new undertaking, where in past centuries in France you would have found the government or in England some territorial magnate, in the United States you were sure to find an association. We need to recapture that spirit of nongovernmental, civil-society potential.

In *Democracy in America*, published in 1835, the French political writer Alexis de Tocqueville wrote of the New World and its burgeoning democratic order. As he observed:

> The Americans combine the notions of Christianity and of liberty so intimately in their minds, that it is impossible to make them conceive the one without the other; and with them this conviction does not spring from that barren traditionary faith which seems to vegetate in the soul rather than to live. . . . Despotism may govern without faith, but liberty cannot. How is it possible that society should escape destruction if the moral tie is not strengthened in proportion as the political tie is relaxed? And what can be done with a people who are their own masters if they are not submissive to the Deity?

From the perspective of a detached social scientist, Tocqueville related his travels through observing the market revolution, western expansion, and Jacksonian democracy radically transforming the fabric of American life. He viewed equality as an emerging and unstoppable force in modern life. He also warned, though, of "Political Consequences of the Social State of the Anglo-Americans," saying "one also finds in the human heart a depraved taste for equality, which impels the weak to want to bring the strong down to their level, and which reduces men to preferring equality in servitude to inequality in freedom."

He added, "Furthermore, when citizens are all almost equal, it becomes difficult for them to defend their independence against the aggressions of power. As none of them is strong enough to fight alone with advantage, the only guarantee of liberty is for everyone to combine forces."

Tocqueville warned that modern democracy might be adept at inventing new forms of tyranny because radical equality could lead to the indifferent materialism of an expanding bourgeoisie and the selfishness of individualism. In such conditions, we lose interest in the future of our descendants and meekly allow ourselves to be led by a despotic force, one all the more powerful because it does not outwardly resemble despotism.

Tocqueville compared a potentially despotic democratic government to a protective parent who wants to keep its citizens "perpetual children" and doesn't break men's wills but rather guides them, presiding over people in the same way as a shepherd looking after a "flock of timid animals." It's not just today's radicals who worry that Americans could become "sheep."

Civilization Has the Tools to Fix the Mess

The safest route out of that fate is to marshal both powerful forces that made the Western world as we know it possible: reason *and* faith. Those two parts are unified in one tradition that has framed Western civilization—sometimes called the Western synthesis—the synthesis between faith and reason. The Judeo-Christian tradition is not a small part of the story; it frames the whole thing. No Western philosopher of note has written independently of that tradition. It simply cannot be ignored. Freedom of conscience, democracy, and human rights come out of this tradition. So do the separation of church and state, modern science and economics, and private property rights. Harvard was founded according to this tradition, with its original motto "Truth for Christ and Church." Boy, have times changed! The same goes for Princeton, Yale, and many other esteemed institutions that have lost their original impulse. More on that later.

So often, we describe the fruits of the West's religious tradition without describing the seeds of faith that made those fruits possible. From the early-modern tradition of opinionated pamphleteers to the movement to abolish slavery, those who lived Western history saw it as the playing out of faith-based commitments, even though some later historians tried hard not to notice. Even if people today question whether we are all children of God, there is no denying that in the West we are all inheritors of this shared Judeo-Christian tradition. When we struggle to communicate with one another and understand differing moral allegiances, why not refer frankly to this deeply rooted, shared common ground?

There is no serious question about whether we have been shaped by the Judeo-Christian tradition. The only debate that matters is whether it has been good or bad for civilization. If morally bad, it should be scrapped. If good, we need to sustain it. In comparison with utopia, a case can be made that our tradition is bad, precisely because human nature is flawed. But in comparison with any other system in the world throughout history, this tradition is nothing short of miraculous. It is what I want to defend. Jean-Jacques Rousseau and Karl Marx both tried to construct a utopian society, but Rousseau could never explain why his "noble savage" went bad in the first place. Rousseau said that civil society and civilization caused the savage to go bad. But why? He had no answer. Marx had an answer: the capitalist and the class system. The owners of capital are morally bad, and Karl Marx is good. Neat.

The only problem with Marx was that he had no ethical system in mind. He had some prophetic judgments but no moral system that he could identify to ground his system. So his economics and ethics failed, but modern academics love him. Why? Because many resent the success of the successful. Forget the evidence that the United States has been and always will be the most generous nation on the face of the earth. Forget that we invent all the lifesaving drugs. The left attacks drug companies for not sharing the drugs but forgets why we have the drugs in the first place: the capitalists.

This is not pride or chauvinism. This is truth. The fact that the truth can cause pain and anger, that it has dark parts and highlights flaws, does not make it less true. In fact, the two primary representatives of this tradition, Socrates for reason and Jesus for religion, were killed on the grounds that they upset others. The prophets bore the same burden. The truth may set us free, but we may be free with a burden. That choice is always yours as an individual. That is the real point of this book.

Dismiss that tradition, and you can rest assured we will be left wondering what went wrong and who is to blame for the loss of our freedom and prosperity. I would rather devote my mental energy to what the Oxford historian Niall Ferguson, in his book *Civilization: The West and the Rest*, calls the most "interesting question" about history: why the West, starting around 1500, became so much more successful than other world societies. It's not as if I were the first to notice this pattern. The emergence of all economies—but especially in the West—during the recent centuries of capitalism and industry can be seen plainly in the encouraging nearby graph of per capita gross domestic product (GDP).

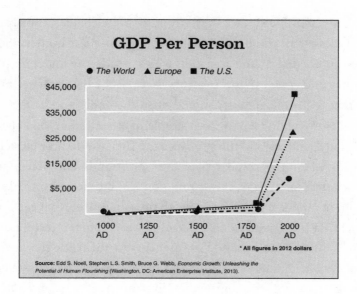

GDP Per Person

● The World   ▲ Europe   ■ The U.S.

$45,000

$35,000

$25,000

$15,000

$5,000

1000 AD   1250 AD   1500 AD   1750 AD   2000 AD

* All figures in 2012 dollars

Source: Edd S. Noell, Stephen L.S. Smith, Bruce G. Webb, *Economic Growth: Unleashing the Potential of Human Flourishing* (Washington, DC: American Enterprise Institute, 2013).

The chart is inflation adjusted, and it comes from my favorite economist, Deirdre McCloskey. To my friends on the left who want to see an index of well-being and not just GDP growth, be aware that the two are highly correlated. A country with high GDP has good health, long life spans, high education levels, and all the "goods" that make for a happy life.

For most of human history, ordinary people in every nation were overtaxed and compelled to serve a ruling class, never earning more than $1,000 a year per person.[21] Not until free markets emerged did we see the drastic hockey-stick-type run-up in our ability to produce and earn high incomes. The wealth that has been created by this great unleashing of human capital is now seen as a source of revenue for the left's pet projects. I find it fascinating how those who bash capitalism are against the only thing that allows us to have good lives.

You also find this idea in the immigration debate. Some say that we are less than compassionate for not opening our borders. Some say walls are bad. So the very folks who are suffering under despotic regimes and socialist governments that reject capitalism are arguing that the evil capitalists should open the doors and let 8 billion people in. Wouldn't it have been simpler if other nations had opened their borders to capital thirty years ago? They would now be rich.

But when government oversteps its bounds and starts picking winners and losers, rewarding political cronies with the taxed wealth of others, it can be easy to fall into a narrative that each time something bad happens, only bigger government can restore order to the system. Nothing could be further from the truth. It is government's growing interference in the free market that has stunted our capacity for exponential growth. Government expansion comes at the expense of the private sector. History has proven that you cannot tax and regulate a country into prosperity. In fact, our modern world was made possible by a change in mind-set that respected and valued—and encouraged—trade and innovation. That's the mind-set that made America great. That's the mind-set we need now.

I'll outline Ferguson's six-part explanation—the "killer apps" that enabled this cultural success—in a later chapter. There's a big happy story to be told here, in which I'm just one small character; but not everyone wants to hear the tale, especially if it threatens to alter the status quo in Washington, DC.

chapter two
WHY I RAN

I ran for office because Washington, DC, is broken. The economy is broken, the rule of law is broken, the health care system is broken, and we are going farther and farther into debt every day. I am an economist, and I wanted to go to that troubled city to fix these problems. Together with my fellow members of the House Freedom Caucus, I'm giving it a shot. We're up against a deeply ingrained culture of cronyism and deal making, but in this chapter I sketch a philosophy that has much deeper roots and may yet prevail.

The free-market system has made our nation the envy of the world. The United States is the richest and most powerful nation on earth. If you are an American, you are blessed. But we are losing the fundamentals, and our foundations are cracking. Take a look at this graph of the federal government's debt. Within a few short years we're on track to match the debt levels we experienced in the dark days of World War II, but most of the political establishment still shows no interest in changing course.

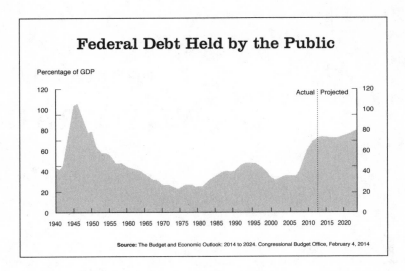

The establishment's tone deafness created an opportunity for me to run on a back-to-basics set of conservative principles that was perfectly in line with the six main values the Virginia Republican Party has espoused since 1975:

1. That the **free enterprise** system is the most productive supplier of human needs and economic justice.
2. That all individuals are entitled to **equal rights**, justice, and opportunities and should assume their responsibilities as citizens in a free society.
3. That **fiscal responsibility** and budgetary restraints must be exercised at all levels of government.
4. That the federal government must preserve individual liberty by observing **constitutional limitations**.
5. That peace is best preserved through a **strong national defense**.
6. That **faith** in God, as recognized by our Founding Fathers, is essential to the moral fiber of the nation.

Something like that basic creed is at least paid lip service by half the Republicans running for office. The difference with me is, I actually believe it. I know many people say the committed conservatives in Congress are the problem, as if everyone else just wants to "get things done" and knows automatically what that should entail. The fact is, there are all sorts of divisions and factions within Congress. Why not use something like the basic Republican Creed above as the playbook all congressional Republicans use? We'll still have our differences, but we won't be nearly as adrift. Creating unity on those core values is both the right thing to do and good strategy. I believe emphasizing a version of that creed would tap into the most deeply held and broadly shared values in our civilization and allow the creation of the ultimate "big tent."

But let's make it even simpler. We can further abbreviate that creed by underscoring three fundamental issues that I will explore more fully in this book. I'm not exactly the only one who owes his success to those factors. We all do, as I will explain.

Three grand themes produced our greatness:

1. The Judeo-Christian **moral tradition**.
2. The **rule of law** and the philosophical values that produced the Constitution of the United States of America.
3. The **free-market system**. That doesn't mean just saying you are pro–big business. Big businesses alone do not constitute free markets. Plenty of them are more than happy to collude with politicians as long as they get a piece of the $4 trillion DC has to throw around—or maybe the opportunity to help craft regulations that hurt their rivals.

Moral Tradition

I think most people want to do the right thing, but we have allowed politicians—and the lobbyists, donors, and activists who influence them—to create an environment in which many people are *afraid* to do the right thing. CEOs and state representatives have told me that they would like to follow the same principles I do, but they fear retaliation from regulators and establishment politicians. There comes a time when someone must step up to provide true leadership and think beyond the next election cycle. Some things are longer lasting than that. Some things are eternal.

Rule of Law

Everyone is equal under the law.

For centuries the idea that the law should apply to all people in the same way has underscored the Judeo-Christian concept of a higher moral law (as we will see in the following chapters). Anything else rightly causes us to react with alarm. Yet Congress routinely exempts its own members from regulations the rest of the country must comply with, including Obamacare. A midnight amendment to the STOCK Act shortly before I was elected permitted *relatives* of members of Congress to engage in insider trading based on congressional knowledge of pending regulations, even as most Americans are subjected to ever stricter insider trading rules. The members' special seat of power allows their relatives to reap profits even in the current state of the economy while our retirement accounts, IRAs, and 401(k)s wither.

Do the American people still have equal treatment under the law? Do we really have equal justice for all? Do we even have true representation if constituents can rarely meet with their members of Congress, who may meet only with the ruling class?

We must ask whether amnesty for illegal immigrants—flagrantly disregarding the many people who have waited in line for months or years for their chance to become US citizens—is truly the rule of law or a chaotic loss of control and national sovereignty.

The government can exert control over the whole population when it wants to, though. Witness the NSA's blatantly unconstitutional universal surveillance. That can't be squared with the Constitution's assurance that people suspected of no crime cannot be arbitrarily subject to searches and seizures without a warrant. There have to be limits on government or it will regulate all things at all times on a whim. And that's not a bad description of how government treats the economy, which we'll get to in a moment.

Before we do, I should stress that I believe in a strong national defense—some expenses are necessary—but I also believe we cannot be the police force for the entire planet. We must constantly be on guard against the unnecessary use of our military. We treasure those who serve because they fight for our liberty, and their lives should not be lightly thrown away for causes unrelated to that all-important mission. For example, US military action in the complex civil war in Syria would be a mistake, and our indecision and poor decision-making process regarding the conflict has been an embarrassment and weakened us internationally.

Free-market System

I stand for free markets, not "too big to fail." Not TARP or bailouts to China, big banks, Wall Street cronies, and government bureaucrats. I don't want to be in Washington to pick winners and losers in the marketplace or to vote for expensive government projects such as the "bridge to nowhere" in Alaska. I could go on and on for two hundred pages, so for a good summary see former Senator

Tom Coburn's periodic lists of pork-barrel projects. The government pretends it is the necessary counterweight to the immorality and recklessness of institutions such as Wall Street megafirms, yet after the financial crisis, no one went to jail. Instead, the biggest crooks have stayed in both the Democrats' and Republicans' Rolodexes.

Regulation is killing the little guy. Every part of your home and business is regulated in minute detail. Ask the small businessman and the small banker whether we really have free markets. Big firms can afford the lawyers and lobbyists necessary to form cozy relationships with regulators, while the small guys and gals go bankrupt. I have heard big lobbyists actually brag about putting the small guys out of business. It's not funny, and it has to change. Regulation now costs about $1.8 trillion in an $18 trillion economy.[1]

I believe in sound economic policy. I believe in living within our means. I believe in balanced budgets. Instead, the debt ceiling has been increased nearly every year this century—even before the financial crisis of 2008. It's a bipartisan problem. The debt went up from $4 trillion to $9 trillion under George W. Bush and then doubled again under Barack Obama.[2] If putting up with this state of affairs—and passing the debt onto future generations—isn't a case of shoddy morals affecting public policy, I don't know what is. And politicians aren't just letting this happen passively. With their debt ceiling increases and even their passage of bills meant to alter the "sequester" agreement, they're tempering with budget cuts that were intended to happen by default, the closest thing to fiscal sobriety Washington can now summon up.

By contrast with the clarity of these principles, my first year in Washington presented me with a few big victories and constant frustration, as it does for other freedom-oriented legislators. The free market is no longer free, and the rule of law is under attack. President Obama has made the issuing of executive orders—on guns, amnesty, health care, and more—his daily routine. Still, my local paper, the *Richmond Times-Dispatch*, ran a piece called "Dave Brat: 'Troublemaker' Carving out Space in Congress" a year after I went to Washington. It was an indication that I was at least putting the establishment on notice that those of us opposed to waste and corruption weren't going away anytime soon.

The original logic behind our republic was that government is best done at the state level, but now everything is forced on us by the lawmakers in Washington, DC. Medicaid expansion, for instance, is dictated to states by DC. Amnesty for illegal immigrants is next. And the federal government has nearly started another war in Syria.

If this trend continues, this great nation could yet fail, and I think voters sent me to DC to act now to make changes, not talk about changes twenty years from now. We don't have that much time. My original congressional campaign was all about returning the power to the people, including the constituents of the Seventh Congressional District of Virginia—not by seeing how much pork I can send them but by making DC as irrelevant to their everyday lives as possible.

Unfortunately, many Americans have been lulled into thinking that all "conservative" and "business-oriented" Washingtonians are speaking on behalf of basic American values. Usually, I'm afraid, they're using your trust—and the political rhetoric you respect—just to get their piece of the Washington pie. I was fascinated by a *Wall Street Journal* article called "A Business Short List for Growth" that appeared in early 2014, a few months prior to my election. Written by the CEO of AT&T, the piece was a mix of tax and regulatory changes that would be great for *his* bottom line but showed little concern for the growth of the US economy as a whole. Naturally, he had recently become the chairman of the Business Roundtable, which, just like its close partner the Chamber of Commerce, cares about a list of specific businesses but not much for the property rights and free markets that allow *everyone* to do business.

Businesses like the ones those trade groups represent are also of course big donors to members of Congress. Little wonder that many of them pursue piecemeal agendas of subsidies and targeted regulatory relief that don't do much for the competitors of their donors or the rest of America.

Instead of defending simple free-market principles, there are four major goals that our crony-capitalist, half-business/half-government ruling class really cares about:

1. "Fiscal stability" in DC, meaning "kicking the can" of budget and debt reform farther down the road to avoid any pain or disruption while the current crop of politicians and CEOs is in place.
2. "Business tax reform," meaning that business will get lower rates but you won't necessarily.
3. "Expanded trade," meaning DC's help, through institutions such as the still thriving Export-Import Bank, with promoting big businesses' efforts overseas.
4. "Fixing the immigration system," which I promise you almost always means amnesty for low-paid illegal workers, in turn leading to:
   a. Lower wages for low-skilled American workers;

b. Taxpayers picking up the costs of education, health care, and welfare while big business pays lower wages to the recipients of those services; and

c. Increased competition for your kids in the job market.

If the crony capitalists—the establishment—were really concerned about the issues that threaten the US economy as a whole, maybe the bullet points on their agenda would look more like a list of solutions to these problems:

1. Debt of $19 trillion
2. Budgets of $4 trillion per year
3. Unfunded programs of over $100 trillion
4. Federal Reserve money printing presses on high gear
5. Fannie Mae and Freddie Mac and the other government-made causes of recurring financial crises

In theory, companies could—and should—expand beyond the boundaries of any one country while retaining their allegiance to American-style free-market ground rules. They should also be able to become large and influential without violating any competitors' property rights. Too often in practice, though, companies believe they can flourish in any environment—domestic or foreign, regulated or unregulated—as long as they are well connected and able to game the rules in their own favor. The original American rules of the market get forgotten.

In contrast, the rules I stand for are pretty simple. The principles I mentioned above—faith, constitutionalism, and markets—aren't just talk. They're a good program for governing.

chapter three

POLICY AND REALITY

How would you like to send someone to Congress to bring both economics and ethics to DC? I asked voters when I ran. That resonated with them. But I sure didn't pretend I could fix things overnight. I can't. Let me explain.

Each year President Obama releases a proposed budget of $4 trillion, about a quarter of that in deficit spending.[1] We hardly even debate the details of the budget-substitute resolutions our system of government now relies on, yet about a quarter of our spending is done with money we don't have. And that's framing the dilemma in a relatively painless short-term way, ignoring our long-term liabilities, such as the duty to fund Medicare and Social Security. This chapter outlines some of the ways business as usual in DC flies in the face of the philosophical principles outlined earlier.

My first several weeks as a member of the House of Representatives showed me how ugly the whole process of governing can be and why it's important to remember that the real battle is an eternal one, not one that will be settled by the next fiscal year. I say this in spite of the fact that another surprise waiting for me was the realization that everyone in Congress is actually very nice to one another. No, really!

I entered Congress in late 2014, just as my fellow legislators were wrestling with a leviathan catchall spending bill nicknamed the "cromnibus"—for "continuing resolution omnibus." As an economics professor turned politician, I see how painfully economically shortsighted politicians are, but I'll admit that current federal government spending levels sometimes seem like a glimpse of eternity. The perpetual "continuing resolutions" are basically a slapdash, last-minute way of rubber-stamping the prior spending levels on nearly every program.

That's terrible for the republic but great for legislators hoping to duck any tough decisions or come up with any fresh ideas, no matter how bad the future looks. In the end, I was one of only sixteen members to vote against the rule permitting the cromnibus to circumvent the usual House budgeting rules. In doing so, I broke two of the informal rules of being a member of the House: never vote against a rule and never vote last. If there's one thing that annoys most members more than ideological differences, it's blocking the easy, lazy route to consensus.

You may not be surprised to hear me complain about the federal budget, given my econ background and the fact that radio host Mark Levin called me "the litmus test for conservatives." You might be more surprised to hear that I have a strong interest in theology and received a master's in that field from Princeton Theological Seminary. That's why, a few weeks after the glimpse of hell on Earth that was the cromnibus, I was more than happy to issue a statement celebrating Dr. Martin Luther King, Jr., a figure not always associated with conservatives. As I said then, "Dr. King was not only a reverend, but also held a PhD in theology; he was intimately familiar with how the Judeo-Christian tradition was the foundation for this grand experiment we call America."

These are my twin themes and two important parts of the story of America's success and the success of Western civilization in general: economic sense and a firm foundation in faith. These intertwined elements of Western tradition have been essential to our survival, and they can still guide our future if we act before our cultural history is forgotten.

Battling the Budget Beast

It's not as if my party doesn't make efforts to fix Washington's fiscal mess.

In the spring of 2015, with the federal government about $18 trillion in debt[2] and getting in deeper all the time (something former chairman of the Joint Chiefs of Staff Admiral Mike Mullen called "the single biggest threat to our national security"[3]), Republicans presented a budget that would balance future federal budgets— match spending to current revenues the way sane businesses and families routinely do—within ten years. It was a budget plan that would fully repeal Obamacare and allow for alternatives that actually lower costs and a budget that would reform entitlement programs to support those in need, prevent fraud, and ensure that those programs are financially sustainable so they are available for future generations.

We suggested $5.5 trillion in spending reductions over the next decade, spending roughly $43.2 trillion instead of the currently projected $48.6 trillion.[4] Both numbers sound gigantic, but this plan would have reformed government spending responsibly while avoiding heavy-handed cuts—protecting key priorities while eliminating waste and modernizing programs.

Repealing Obamacare in its entirety—including all the tax increases, job-killing regulations, and mandates that go with it—would save our nation more than $2 trillion.[5] Instead of a complex structure of subsidies, mandates, and penalties, the proposed GOP budget would have increased access to affordable health care by expanding choices and flexibility for individuals, families, and businesses. It would empower states—not Washington—to tailor their Medicaid programs to best serve the most vulnerable of their citizens. The budget also proposed to reform Medicare to harness the power of consumer choice that made the prescription drug plan under Medicare Part D so popular, and it provided oversight and reforms for the terrible bureaucracy at the Department of Veterans Affairs.

By consolidating redundant programs, shoring up the major entitlements Social Security and Medicare, and reining in runaway spending on programs such as food stamps, the budget provided a glimpse of a more rational Washington where serious effort was being made to avoid the slow-motion economic catastrophe caused by our current government spending levels.

Some of the most damaging costs of government that I observed in my first year in Washington couldn't be gauged in budget dollars alone. There are the endless regulations foisted on US businesses, which make it harder to function, render production more expensive, and in the end produce a high price tag for the consumer. The Republican budget proposal sought to deal with that as well.

We noted that since President Obama took office in January 2009, the federal government has issued more than 468,500 pages of regulations.[6] The overwhelming amount and burdensome nature of these regulations are hurting our economy. The National Association of Manufacturers estimates the total cost of regulations to be as high as $2.03 trillion per year and says that a "disproportionate share" of the compliance costs fall on small businesses.[7] This translates into fewer job opportunities for American workers and much higher costs for consumers.

Since it is the average American consumer we're worried about, the budget also sought to eliminate several corporate welfare programs, a stab at stopping cronyism. Washington should not be in the business of picking the winners and losers of our economy in the private sector. The best way to ensure a vibrant and strong economy is to allow innovators to thrive based on merit and consumer demand for their products and services, not on the powerful friends they have in Washington.

Hardworking American families are struggling as average hourly wages are barely keeping pace with inflation. Real median household income is just under $52,000[8]—one of the lowest levels since the mid-1990s—and an unhealthy percentage of the workforce has dropped out of the labor market.[9] Between the thousands of pages of ineffective and overburdening regulations, the millions of unemployed workers, and the trillions of dollars in out-of-control spending, it is obvious that we have trillion-dollar problems that call for trillion-dollar solutions. That reformist budget—with its serious and commonsense proposals—represented a solid first step toward reining in uncontrolled federal spending, turning our economy around, and creating an environment that will spur job creation and higher wages for all Americans.

Naturally, threatened with the likelihood of a presidential veto and little support from the Democrats in Congress, we ended up with another hasty catchall spending bill like the cromnibus that was being fought over when I arrived.

The Victories That Keep You Going

I'm pleased to report that not all activity on the Hill in Washington is futile.

My first year gave me a chance to warn about a "border security bill" that was really a Trojan horse for amnesty, entrusting all border enforcement power to the president. I later coauthored a letter with Senator Jeff Sessions (R-AL) urging serious defense of the borders. (That has been an uphill battle. I think it's odd yet telling that the 2016 Republican response to the president's State of the Union address by South Carolina Governor Nikki Haley was basically as much an attack on Donald Trump as on the president's speech, if not more so. It's another example of the disconnect between GOP voter and GOP donor.)

But there are ways to work within the system and make small advancements, even if the system is rigged. For example, I've worked with physicians in my district to improve Medicare reimbursement to doctors without busting the budget.

Given the necessary checks and balances in our system, sometimes the best you can do is hope that the House will vote for something that can pave the way for a later bill that would be supported by the Senate and signed by the president, even if this isn't quite the year the bill becomes law. I happily voted for the Death Tax Repeal Act of 2015, which would permanently end the federal estate tax's choke hold over American families. The tax, which currently seizes up to 40 percent of a person's property upon death, is often levied on property that has been taxed once already. Regardless of the wealth of those who are hit with it, the tax is just plain immoral, another mingling of economic and ethical misrule. Our government shouldn't punish those who subscribe to the American dream.

Central to that ideal is the underlying principle that through entre-
preneurship, thrift, and tenacity, people should be able to leave their
children a better quality of life than perhaps they had.

Speaking of morality meeting markets, I also voted for the Prevent Targeting at the IRS Act, which authorizes the IRS to terminate
employees who target individuals or groups based on their political beliefs. The bill, had it become law, would have explicitly added
the targeting of taxpayers because of politics to a list of so-called
ten deadly sins that result in the firing of misbehaving IRS employees. The really scary part is that they might have just been following
orders in making it harder for conservative groups to get and keep
their nonprofit status. President Obama seems to operate with a de
facto "enemies list" not unlike the one Nixon was said to keep.

The IRS's targeting of political groups is beyond reprehensi-
ble and contradicts everything our country stands for. Our First
Amendment rights guarantee that no one can be punished for his
or her political opinions. If being philosophically opposed to the
big-government status quo is now to be treated as a crime or a tax
violation, I'm going to be in a great deal of trouble in the years ahead.
But fighting big government is my mission.

You Almost Wonder Whose Side
the Government Is On

There are times when what Washington regards as business as
usual—the sorts of things that sail through easily in those big
catchall spending bills—seems insane rather than routine. I agree
that the military is an appropriate and vital function of the federal
government, but I partnered with Representative Mo Brooks (R-AL)
to stop an amendment in a huge defense bill that would actually

have paid for illegal aliens to serve in our military. At a time when tens of thousands of US citizens are being downsized from the military or turned away by recruiters—and there are legitimate concerns about our enemies infiltrating our forces—why is letting illegals serve a priority? You almost have to wonder sometimes: Which nation does the federal government protect exactly?

Yet the amendment, which passed on a poorly attended late-night 33–30 vote, encourages the secretary of defense to declare that illegal immigrants categorized under Obama's Deferred Action for Childhood Arrivals (DACA) are "vital" to the United States' national interest and eligible to enlist in the US armed forces.

As Mo Brooks and I asked in a statement at the time of our bill aimed at getting rid of the amendment, "Do members of the House Armed Services Committee who voted for this amendment really believe that these are jobs Americans won't do? It is unconscionable that certain members of Congress seek to use America's military as a bargaining chip in a bid to cement the president's unconstitutional amnesty actions—adding the amendment to the 'must pass' National Defense Authorization Act, a bill that is intended to authorize essential programs for our military. We can't speak for other Congressmen, but, as for ourselves, we were elected to promote and protect the interests of American citizens, not illegal immigrants."

Given the crisis at our nation's border, across which tens of thousands of children are pouring into our country illegally, it is mind-boggling that Congress would consider a policy that encourages even more illegal immigrants to unlawfully cross US borders. Yet so strong is the commitment to open borders on the Democratic side of the aisle that members of Congress are willing to endorse a cycle of perpetual amnesty for illegal immigrants and betray struggling young Americans who wish to serve in our country's armed forces in one fell swoop.

You almost begin to wonder whether the United States is more imperiled by foreign governments or our own.

Defending the Most Defenseless

If Congress has been unwilling to protect our borders and fighting forces, it is hardly surprising that the unborn—who after all don't vote yet—tend to be dismissed by many legislators. The nature of the soul has been debated for centuries, but science aligns with faith in observing that fetuses can feel pain at a sufficiently advanced point in gestation. It may be easy for proabortion forces to dismiss the unborn as mere tissue, but when the unborn have nerves and can suffer, even the most liberal conscience may be pricked.

With that hope in mind, I was proud to cosponsor the Pain-Capable Unborn Child Protection Act, which passed the House and, if it is eventually signed by the president, would prohibit late-term abortions after twenty weeks, the point at which growing scientific evidence confirms babies feel pain in the womb. The bill also provided exceptions for cases of rape, incest, or when the life of the mother is threatened, a humane caveat motivated in part by the view that moral culpability then falls upon the rapist. Of course, some in the proabortion camp have tried to make such exceptions out to be mere hypocrisy or inconsistency. I'd call it moral nuance, something the proabortion side often lacks. Sixty percent of Americans—a cross section of Republicans, Democrats, and independents—say they support such legislation.

Despite all the criticism the religious right gets from the left and the media these days, the truth is that the United States is only one of seven countries in the world that allow elective abortions after twenty weeks. If left-leaning continental Europe can place sensible restrictions on abortion, I think we can too.

Budgets No One Loves

Other battles from my eye-opening first year in Washington have included the House's passage of the Regulatory Integrity Protection Act, needed to stop an Environmental Protection Agency regulation that could ultimately force district farmers and families to seek permits to use water on their own lands. Many farmers and landowners were preparing for the EPA to mandate that they fence in ponds and ditches on their properties because of the agency's pending "Waters of the United States" rule, a plan to radically redefine the scope of the waters the federal government can regulate. Prior to the proposal, the term "Waters of the United States" traditionally governed "navigable waters," such as those navigated by boats or ships. The EPA—which must be thinking of boats much, much smaller than the ones I see in Virginia's ports—wants "navigable waters" to mean drainage ditches, farm ponds, and even seasonally wet areas. So if a heavy rain deposited a stream of water on one's property, under certain circumstances, the federal government could regulate it. That's crazy.

It's also a bit crazy that we need something like the Hezbollah International Financing Prevention Act, which imposes US sanctions on financial institutions that intentionally facilitate transactions for the terrorist organization Hezbollah or its affiliates. With the Obama administration racing to open up relations and trade with Iran, it's worth reminding one and all that the US Department of the Treasury designates the Iran-supported, anti-Israel Hezbollah as a terrorist organization. We should be doing everything we can to cut off the flow of money to and reduce the impact of such an organization. But in DC, even matters of life and death have a way of falling through the bureaucratic cracks.

In my first year I also voted for the Restoring Americans' Healthcare Freedom Reconciliation Act of 2015, intended to rein in some of the unreasonable side effect costs of Obamacare, and a bill to protect financial advice to and lower planning costs for those entering retirement.

Dishearteningly, it's not usually the commonsense reform bills that become law. Somehow, in the midst of the wrangling over the big omnibus bill we faced on my one-year anniversary on the Hill, Congress brought back to life the crony-capitalist Export-Import Bank, a New Deal relic that was originally created to subsidize US exports during the Great Depression. As is characteristic of government programs, the bank outlived its purpose until conservatives stood with the American taxpayers to allow its charter to expire in the summer of 2015—after which it was nonetheless renewed in November of that year, amid intense lobbying from industry.

It was a sad day in Washington when instead of deliberating over how to reduce our $19 trillion debt or tackle the almost $100 trillion in eventual unfunded liabilities we face, we revived a defunct government program for the rich and well connected.

Even Paul Ryan called the new budget a "crap sandwich"; outgoing Speaker Boehner left us with trillion-dollar deficits as far as the eye can see, and Congress quickly seconded the idea.

As an economist, I support free trade and equal protection under the law, so I oppose special privileges and Washington planning the economy. Just as then-Senator Barack Obama said in 2008, the Export-Import Bank is "little more than a fund for corporate welfare." Yet I watched forty-two Republicans band together using a procedural move called a discharge petition, which amounts to giving Democratic leadership control of the House floor, to restore this program for special interests, not ordinary Americans' interests.

To accommodate such countless unnecessary bits of spending, naturally Congress also voted in late 2015 to suspend the spending caps that Republicans had previously fought so hard to put into place, not only raising the debt ceiling but actually suspending it until March 15, 2017. In effect, it gave three of the five negotiators—Senate Minority Leader Harry Reid, Speaker John Boehner, and President Barack Obama—control over the budget process even after they leave office.

Fighting amid Bureaucracy

While I remain in Washington, I'll keep fighting to stop things such as arrogant government, and I'll support institutions such as the Congressional Budget Office and the Joint Committee on Taxation. Not all government agencies are horrible, and they should be commended for the high-quality, nonpartisan analysis they provide. Their cost and revenue estimates are an indispensable part of my process for reviewing legislation. However, most of their cost estimates are incomplete: they don't contain the costs of debt service. I have introduced the Cost Estimates Reform Act to include the costs of added debt in CBO and JCT analysis to provide members of Congress with more accurate estimates to help inform their decisions.

Whether Congress is paying for basic infrastructure or putting more serious resources into screening Syrian refugees for people with terror ties, there are programs most Americans can agree on. The process would probably result in more consensus if the entire government were subject to greater transparency and there were more time to read bills, and I've voted for bills aimed at those rational goals.

By voting for measures such as protecting small businesses from unreasonable regulations and Americans from covert tax hikes, I keep pushing in the general direction of limited government and freer markets. For the first time ever, both chambers of Congress approved a major repeal of Obamacare during my first year, which is the sort of victory that gives a small bit of hope for the future, even though President Obama can be counted on to veto any attack on his signature legislation.

Obama won't always be in office, and it's important even when facing legislative setbacks to continue fighting and remembering which direction we're trying to move. Ultimately, it's a battle far longer in the making—and likely with far longer to go before being resolved—than any one-year legislative calendar. Throughout these fights I try to recall the principles that can be traced back to the very start of our civilization. I had those same principles in mind even on the day of my primary election victory, which started this whole adventure in the messy business of governing.

Let me show you just how those old principles guide the new kid on the Capitol Hill block and how they got me here.

chapter four
DAVE VS. GOLIATH

*It's not about Dave Brat winning tonight. It's about
returning the country to constitutional principles. It's about
returning the country to Judeo-Christian principles. And it's
about returning this country to free-market principles.*

That's what I told the crowd when I won the Republican Party
primary for Virginia's Seventh Congressional District in June 2014,
setting me on the path to election to Congress five months later. In
this chapter I will outline how the chaos in Washington is the opposite of the philosophy I went to that city to fight for.

If I stay true to my principles, I must admit that there are at least
some members of Congress who are fighting against bloated budgets, chaos on our borders, and the gradual replacement of a society
of moral rules by government regulation. It's a fight not just against
one political party but against detached elites in both.

As many commentators noted at the time, my victory in the
primary was in many ways a bigger shock than my victory in the
general election. "This is the political version of the San Francisco
earthquake," said the *Rothenberg & Gonzales Political Report*. "It

came out of nowhere." By sticking to strong conservative principles, I defeated a prominent, well-established rival, the first sitting
House majority leader to be defeated since the creation of that office
in 1899.

Often, complacent members of the establishment in both parties
offer sound bites and hope the public will consume them, Instead,
I talked to voters during the campaign and discovered that unlike
establishment power brokers, nearly all ordinary Americans say the
country is on the wrong track. The establishment politicians don't
share or even notice the average American's sense of crisis. That was
the key to my victory, and I hope I make a big enough difference on
Capitol Hill to deserve that victory.

The conservative pundit William Kristol and the left-wing
magazine the *Nation* agreed that my success was due to attacking
Republican cronyism, injecting a note of populism. Ryan Lizza of
the *New Yorker* called me "the Elizabeth Warren of the right," and
although Warren isn't exactly my role model, in this case I'll take it
as a compliment.

From Economics to Theology and Back

Like Elizabeth Warren, I have been a college professor, though
not a liberal one, remember. Long before that, I was born in
Detroit. I grew up in Alma, Michigan, right in the middle of the
"mitten," if you're familiar with the shape of the state. My babysitters
were farmers. In the eighth grade, my dad moved us to Minneapo-
lis, Minnesota. He's a doctor and my mom is a nurse, and Dad took
a position in that city running an HMO. It was a rough point in my
life to move because high school was about to start and I was making key friendships. But looking back on it, the move was probably a
good thing because it taught me a lot about life and transitions at an

early age. I enjoyed Minnesota. I loved sports and became the tennis captain in high school, and I played the trumpet in the band and in the Minnesota Youth Symphony and Greater Twin Cities Youth Symphony. Then I attended Hope College in Holland, Michigan, a small liberal arts school with a fairly strong religious affiliation to the Dutch Reformed denomination, which is much like the Presbyterians.

I received a great education with three amazing mentors: a philosopher, a world religions professor, and a minister, who all took a personal interest in me and helped me to develop as a human being. I majored in business, almost minored in religion, and went from Hope College to work at Arthur Andersen in Detroit. The accounting firm sent me to Chicago for about a year and a half. I had the complete package: a life lived at the top of a high-rise, overlooking Lake Michigan and Lincoln Park. I loved the people at work, but I was basically coding in COBOL and doing distribution system work. Soon I discovered that that was not my calling.

I applied to Princeton Theological Seminary in New Jersey, and it was the best move I ever made. In the words of Robert Frost, I took the road less traveled, and it made all the difference. It was pretty funny at the Arthur Andersen send-off for folks leaving at the end of the year. Most were going to Harvard Business School or Stanford. When I said I was headed to Princeton Seminary, a lot of people got a kick out of that. But later some of them chatted with me behind closed doors and confessed that they thought about doing similar things with their own lives.

So I went off to Princeton Seminary for the best education of my life. I intended to graduate and probably become a college professor in the area of systematic theology. But when I attended Wesley Theological Seminary in Washington, DC, for a while, I had a professor who was writing on economics and ethics—in one book. In my stump speech, that combo is usually a lifeline because people understand the challenge and the potential of doing economics and ethics at the same time. It can be rough for most people to think in both those modes at the same time, but then, if you throw in Washington, DC, as a real-life example, their confusion turns into thunderous laughter. I had a background in business and an interest in ethics, and bridging that divide became my calling. Exploring those connections led me into politics.

After Wesley Seminary, I obtained my PhD in economics at the American University, which is right next door to Wesley. (Both have Methodist historical affiliations.) The beauty of being in DC is that you can go to a talk every day and hear experts speak about every aspect of public policy imaginable, including economics. While I was in grad school, I worked for the US Army doing economics and later for the World Bank in its education division in the Philippines, trying to determine how to improve education for children there and creating general lessons for people in developing economies. I loved making new friends from all over the globe with a similar passion for economics and making the world a better place.

Near the end of my PhD program, I met Laura, the best thing that has happened in my life. We dated and married, then moved to Ashland, Virginia, where I became a professor of economics at Virginia's Randolph-Macon College and taught for eighteen years. Laura and I had applied only to liberal arts schools near her home in Washington State, my home in Michigan, and the DC area. I was lucky that Randolph-Macon wanted an economist with an interest in ethics. I also had an interest in teaching third-world economic development as well as international trade and economic justice. Eventually I became the chair of economics and business there and served in that capacity for six years. I ran the ethics minor program and worked on the "ethics bowl" program, which is a debate competition that highlights ethics across all the private colleges in Virginia. BB&T offered me a grant to run a moral foundations of capitalism program, combining the areas of economics and ethics, for about six years. So the line of thought that began back in seminary continues to this day and is one of the reasons I ran for political office.

While at Randolph-Macon, I volunteered for Senator Walter Stosch for six or seven years, and for three years I worked at the Virginia General Assembly, primarily on education issues, including vouchers and creative ways to help kids with disabilities. I also worked for a few years in the area of higher education on STEM (science, technology, engineering, and mathematics). For many years I met educational leaders from across the state. So when the newspapers asked, "Who is Dave Brat? He came out of nowhere!," that is not exactly true. I knew many kids in the area and most of the delegates, senators, and leaders in my region, and I worked downtown at the General Assembly and with the Richmond Metropolitan Authority, which connected several of the counties. In addition, I was president of the Virginia Association of Economists. I actually worked in economic consulting for a few years with a friend, too. When the time came to dive into politics, I had a pretty rich background to draw from, including running for state delegate a few years prior to my US House run.

The glimpse of how things work that I got running for state delegate really motivated me to dive into local affairs and try to fix some of the machine politics in our area. What I've learned about history in general and economics in particular suggests that core conservative principles really work. They aren't just wishes, impossible ideals, or campaign slogans. History provides us with hard evidence, if today's politicians bothered to pay attention. This book is an effort to remind them and citizens alike about that evidence.

My insurgent campaign received a big boost from the talk radio firebrand Laura Ingraham. She claims that there are only two times so far this century when she felt confident a candidate she'd only just gotten to know was going to win, once with Barack Obama and once with me. In fact, thanks to Virginia's open party primaries, I earned votes from Democrats, some of whom might even have voted for Barack Obama in the past.

Some critics will say that my victory was due partly to those crossover voters trying to undermine the Republican establishment, but I think I have a broader appeal than that. Indeed, I imagine that most Americans, whether they think of themselves as liberals or conservatives, believe some version of the basic principles found in the Virginia Republican Creed and that our most esteemed political leaders have as well, from the tax-cutting anticommunist John F. Kennedy to the tax-cutting anticommunist Ronald Reagan. Those six principles (free enterprise, equal rights, fiscal responsibility, constitutional limitations, strong national defense, and faith) provide a good agenda for helping all American citizens, not just my Seventh District constituents.

But if some of those voting for me were only trying to do damage to the cause of conservatism, all I can say is "Sorry, leftists, you've helped put a principled conservative in office." Not that I mean to sound ungrateful.

Into the Congressional Turmoil

My defeated primary opponent announced that he would retire from Congress the following month, enabling the Virginia governor to declare a special election in November. If I won,

I would immediately go to Congress to fill the vacancy, instead of having to wait until January to be sworn in with the rest of the new Congress. Fantastic!

The November victory over Democrat Jack Trammell was even more resounding (nearly two to one) than my primary victory, and I was off to Washington, with barely enough time or money to locate an apartment there. An added irony of the general election was that Trammell is a fellow Randolph-Macon professor, though in the sociology department. It would be wrong to draw any sweeping conclusions, but maybe sociologists would benefit from adding more economics to their analysis, much as I benefited from adding econ to my religious studies.

One new economic lesson that confronted me upon arrival in Washington was the chaos that was the "cromnibus," for "continuing resolution omnibus bill," a technical way of saying "the bills by which Washington now perpetually operates by continuing to spend at about the same levels on whatever programs existed before without engaging in any intelligent debate about how to improve things." It used to be considered an emergency spending situation if such a resolution was used as a cheap (or rather, very expensive) substitute for the real budget bills Congress has a constitutional duty to pass. Now it's business as usual. The crisis is permanent, and I was plunged into it as soon as I arrived in the nation's dysfunctional capital.

Since I'm on the House Budget Committee (as well as the Education and Small Business committees), I'm painfully aware of how irrelevant normal budgeting procedures had become in Congress. There isn't much point in the voters even sending representatives, whether establishment or antiestablishment, to Washington if even the House Budget Committee doesn't determine the budget and all spending is effectively decided by the House leadership in collaboration with the president. Something had to change.

In early 2015, I joined about three dozen other members of the House of Representatives to form the House Freedom Caucus, a smaller and more hard-core, pro-limited-government alternative to the larger and more broadly conservative Republican Study Committee. We pressed for greater budgetary restraint and for the much simpler principle that the leadership, particularly then-Speaker John Boehner of Ohio, ought to consult with the rest of the membership when crafting major legislation, at least with its own party, or at the very least with a majority of its own party (a "majority of the majority," as the so-called Hastert Rule puts it).

It was really the stubborn commitment to principle of the Freedom Caucus—the fanaticism, our critics would claim—that drove Boehner's reaffirmation in mid-September 2015 that he would resign, something he had planned to do almost a year earlier but had changed his mind about when no ready, widely agreed upon replacement for him arose. Part of the reason there was no obvious replacement in 2014 was that the Freedom Caucus wouldn't accept just any business-as-usual candidate.

After a period of great confusion, Representative Paul Ryan, three years earlier the Republican nominee for vice president, emerged as a palatable consensus choice for Speaker, but he had no interest in a close, contentious battle for the position. He wisely announced that he would put his name into consideration only if he had the support of three major factions of the House Republicans: the conservative Republican Study Committee, the moderate and establishment-leaning Tuesday Group, and our own conservative-leaning Freedom Caucus.

We were already being denounced in the press as the crazy hard-liners who were making it impossible to "govern," as if rubber-stamping every big-government budget plan and new program were the essence of responsible stewardship of the republic. But we weren't unreasonable and neither was Ryan. Though he didn't receive the unanimous support of the Freedom Caucus, he got the support of a majority of us, and that was enough for him to proceed with some confidence that he'd be able to get his party to work together in the House.

I like Paul Ryan personally and would have happily voted yes for him if he had put his principles and promises down on paper ahead of time. I sent a list of five policy and five process issues for all candidates for leadership. Most filled in and agreed with all ten, but Ryan was under political pressure not to lean one way or the other in a very divided conference, and he would not put pen to paper. So following my own principles, I had to vote no. I had promised my constituents that I would vote only for leaders who promised to follow through on our Virginia Republican Creed, and that is how I operate at home and in DC.

The House Freedom Caucus got Paul Ryan to agree in principle, though without any precise promises, to several reforms that would give ordinary members more say and ordinary Americans more hope of seeing mushrooming budgets and perilous debt reined in, at least a little.

Ryan tentatively agreed to restructure the House Republican Steering Committee to listen more to members, empower committee chairmen, change the rules for their election and a few other troubling House rules, adhere to the majority-of-the-majority Hastert Rule on contentious legislation, including immigration matters, and avoid immigration "reform" measures until after Barack Obama, arguably a radical on the issue, is out of office.

It's not exactly a blood oath to commit the legislature's sacred honor to restoring strict constitutional limits on our leviathan government, but it's a start.

Some Answers in Our Own Past

The deeper, older principles I'm interested in defending are nothing as newfangled as the Hastert Rule or the Freedom Caucus, useful as those are. They are means, like this book, of restarting a dialogue about far older principles—the ones the republic was founded on, which I fear we are drifting from rapidly: individual freedom, limited and constitutional government, and free markets. Yet even those venerated ideas are new compared to the still deeper and older roots of the civilization that gave rise to limited government and free markets, including moral objectivity, which serves as the necessary foundation for them all.

My real thesis in this volume, though, is that those principles are not seriously in doubt. The left cannot really debate them and is thus reduced to doing a mere end run around them—constantly dodging the core issues, insulting critics, seeking short-lived controversies to distract the public, all the while stealthily setting the republic on a dangerous, uncertain path away from the tried and true and toward something that cannot be named.

To get a better handle on what does work—and reveal the disasters that can befall even well-meaning people when they stray from those lessons—we would do well to begin with a tale of two revolutions, the American and the French. Then we will dig deeper and look back to the very start of democracy and Western civilization some two thousand years earlier.

The American and French revolutionaries thought of themselves as brothers. Famous men participated in both movements. Yet one of those revolutions led to the emergence of the most prosperous and free society the earth had ever known. The other, though it is celebrated to this day (especially on the left), led to mass murder, terror, dictatorship, and years of warfare across Europe. Small philosophical errors can have devastating consequences.

That being the case, we should be worried if, nearly two and a half centuries later, our own philosophical foundations are being forgotten in favor of expediency—the Constitution traded for the next cromnibus, as if continually kicking the can down the road can last forever. But take heart: I think much of our current forgetfulness springs from timidity. When we need to sacrifice our founding principles, average citizens become convinced by the left's arguments and sometimes the right's bluster that the principles can be defended and are sufficient to get us through the next crisis. It keeps happening until we have done it so many times that we don't even remember adhering to the principles in the first place.

But if those principles really work as governing guides, not just campaign rhetoric, that's good news. History ceases to be merely a record of horrors (though it certainly is) and becomes the proof that we are on the right track. Or rather, that until fairly recently, at least when we were at our best, we *were* on the right track. As a professor, I need to recognize from time to time when it's necessary to revisit fundamentals. If we do, I think you'll agree that the solution to our current problems—economic instability, moral chaos, unfettered big government—exists and was with us at the founding.

It's a philosophy of governance that inspired me to run for Congress, and if we return to it, it's a philosophy that may spare me the embarrassment of being in Congress as the nation collapses into ruin.

But now let's take a look at how this national experiment started. When examining our country's origins, I shudder that we've fallen so far short of our ideals. I can't help but wonder how Alexander Hamilton, who defended the new Constitution on the grounds of its potential to make the newly independent states fiscally solvent, would have reacted to the cromnibus.

chapter 5

A TALE OF TWO REVOLUTIONS

Two centuries ago, the United States and continental Europe took two very different paths. And for us, that made all the difference. Though I warn you, in this chapter I reveal that we're now veering much closer to the European model and betraying our own founding principles.

After more than 220 years of the federal government's growth, you can't blame the average voter for feeling powerless. Even a well-meaning citizen, reading newspapers and following political developments, would be hard pressed to keep up with every decision made by the various Cabinet-level agencies in Washington, not to mention the backroom dealings that sometimes cause the most important shifts in policy. Government is vast and largely inaccessible, and exerting small-*d* democratic influence over it is tough, certainly much tougher than deciding what contracts to enter into or businesses to collaborate with in your own private life. We have a big fight trying to rein in government.

But things didn't start out this way.

The American revolutionaries were not thinking like modern welfare-state economists when they decided to resist the army of King George III.

They didn't create graphs showing the size of the state, contrasted with the size of the private sector, and then plot the location of the proper amount of freedom for the citizenry. That sounds more like the way most of my fellow economics professors choose a political system. Actually, it still sounds more pragmatic than the way politicians actually make policy. However, the revolutionaries drew upon two forms of lived experience that counted for more than mere calculations, which led them to more philosophically sound conclusions: the constant commercial activity of the New World and the inherited legal traditions of England.

Free markets are not a recent development on this continent. Beginning four hundred years ago, settlers found not only greater religious freedom but vast resources and an escape from Old World regulations. In the seventeenth century, even before the United States was an independent nation, this land had a reputation for rapidly growing populations and fortunes, one it would retain throughout the world, at least until the Great Depression and arguably to this day.

The legal origins of the United States stretch back another four hundred years before the arrival of the Jamestown and Plymouth settlers, though. In a sense, the legal rights of Englishmen, as the colonists understood them, traced back to 1215 and the signing of the Magna Carta by England's King John. We wouldn't recognize the Magna Carta as a broad bill of rights for ordinary citizens, but for the first time it spelled out the limits on a sovereign's power, even if those limits were primarily constraints on what the king could do to the aristocrats. It was a start.

It is no coincidence that four centuries later, in the era of the Glorious Revolution, England would be infused with a political philosophy calling into question the very right of rulers to stay in power if they do not have the approval of the governed.

That same spirit informed the American Revolution nearly a century after England's own revolution. Our Founders were steeped in the writings of British philosophers such as John Locke, who wrote, "being all equal and independent, no one ought to harm another in his life, health, liberty, or possessions."[1] He believed that men have the right to overthrow tyrannical governments that do not respect those boundaries. From the fighting spirit of the *original* Boston Tea Party in 1773 to the sedate rationality that crafted the Constitution fourteen years later, America's message to rulers foreign and domestic has been: there are limits.

It is not really hatred of government—certainly not hatred of a government that remains in its proper sphere—that animates the American people. Rather, it is a love of their own lives and their fellow citizens' lives, as well as the freedom to shape those lives as they choose. Leftists enamored of government look upon a government shackled by constitutional restraints as a sad, pitiable thing. They say, "Think of the good it could accomplish if unleashed!" But if that "good" consists mainly of giving us orders—forcing us to do things we don't want to do and pay for things we don't want to buy—government's expanded freedom of action is our diminishment.

In summary, is freedom good? Is freedom a right? If it is, the government we have now formed is fundamentally violating our most basic rights in a profound way.

Obviously, if left to our own devices, Americans wouldn't just sit around waiting for someone else to take charge and tell us what to do. For four hundred years—since before the Declaration of Independence and even before the Glorious Revolution over in England—this continent has been where people came to do what they wanted to do, get rich in the fashion they dreamed, worship as they chose. The Declaration of Independence was not Jefferson's invention of a creed for people who were rebels and nothing more. Though written in 1776, the Declaration of Independence was an encapsulation of timeless principles that undergirded American freedom and prosperity and could do the same for the world. If we had been especially fortunate, it would have done so long ago in nations around the globe.

But learning takes time, and humanity is still struggling with the lessons of 1776, still uncertain about whether to take them to heart, especially when so many of our intellectuals pretend they know better. There is always the temptation to create a centrally planned order instead of letting people go about their business. Until very recently, Europe was much more prone to fall prey to that temptation than we were.

A Revolution Gone Wrong

Even as the Constitution, rooted in timeless natural law and the evolved traditions of English law, went into effect in 1789 in the United States, France experienced a revolution spawned by more dangerous ideas, including those of the philosopher Jean-Jacques Rousseau.

Before we dig into the philosophical matters below, it is important to note that for much of our history most Americans would have seen no great tension between the laws of God, the laws of nature, and the laws of our own government. My own grandmother viewed the world in this way. There is a unity to it. In its simplest form the natural law can be viewed as the Ten Commandments and the laws of nature that seemed fairly constant to earlier generations. Now, to many, the world seems upside down. Those who call for love are swearing at their opponents on TV. Our culture is in chaos. The notes below will help to show how we got here.

As the historian Niall Ferguson notes, Jean-Jacques Rousseau's book *The Social Contract* (1762) was among the most dangerous books Western civilization ever produced. Man, Rousseau argued, is a "noble savage" who is reluctant to submit to authority. The only legitimate authority he can submit to is the sovereignty of the People—the "General Will."[2] According to Rousseau, that General Will must be supreme. Magistrates and legislators must bow down before it. There can be no "sectional association." There can be no Christianity, which after all implies a separation of powers (the spiritual from the temporal). No doubt freedom is a good thing. But for Rousseau virtue is more important. The General Will should be virtue in action.

What made the conservative theorist Edmund Burke react so violently against Rousseau and the French Revolution? How was he able to foresee the true character of the French Revolution within a year of its outbreak? The real "social contract" for Burke was not Rousseau's pact between the "noble savage" and the "General Will," but a partnership between the present generation and future generations. With astonishing prescience, Burke warned against the utopianism of "the professors." "At the end of every vista" envisioned by the French Revolution, he wrote in the greatest prophecy of the era, "you see nothing but the gallows." The assault (of Rousseau and the French) on institutions, he warned, "would end in a mischievous and ignoble oligarchy" and, ultimately, military dictatorship.[3] In all this, Burke was proven right.

In short, this was the emergence of national planning. The planners know best. They determine the General Will, the common good, call it what you like, but the planners will use coercion to make sure you bow down before it. It is un-freedom.

Ferguson has shown us that the precise nature of the "social contract" does matter in the end, and we might ask ourselves how the social contract Burke proposed is looking at present. How is the "partnership between the present and future generations" faring? Is the rule of law protecting the interests of all people equally? Or are we borrowing heavily at the expense of the future and leaving them the bill? In fact, we are saying that some have more rights than others.

We have become utopian, and the major deception giving this bogus utopia any credence is the $100 trillion pile of entitlements that are currently providing (utopian) benefits at zero interest rates. The fantasy cannot last, and the only issue that matters is if we can protect retirees while avoiding the gallows in the end—or, in present-day terms, a bond default. Plato also argued that the regime following democracy is dictatorship. Weak-minded professors create a world without leadership and values, where all values are equal. But chaos emerges when values do not provide order. And then the dictator is happy to provide order. I hope you can see the analogy to today in Plato's outline.

Rather than recognizing strict limits on government action, Rousseau saw government as a welcome expression of the General Will. In the view of the fanatics who followed Rousseau, restraints upon government such as those embodied in the US Constitution would just get in the way of creating a virtuous republic. (Much the way that the leftist commentator Matthew Yglesias argues today that Hillary Clinton is *admirable* for not letting petty laws get in the way of her doing what she knows needs doing, for being "more comfortable than the average person with violating norms and operating in legal gray areas" and asking "what she can get away with."[4])

In a pattern that at first sounds contradictory but would recur in the liberals of our own time, Rousseau's unlimited view of government was accompanied by a view that individual sentiment should be unfettered as long as citizens were the right sort of individuals, feeling the right sort of sentiments.

With the right early education, Rousseau thought individuals could be created who would not need the shackles of tradition and self-restraint. Hello, Common Core. We need to shape the kids. Notice that national testing has saved history for last. First you do math, science, and English, then history and religion at the end. Once you change the history texts, it is game over. If our contemporary dilemma is one characterized by the substitution of feelings for morals and government intervention for private sector initiative, Rousseau gets a big dose of blame for starting our decline. The result in his own time was the revolutionary Terror, when some forty thousand insufficiently revolutionary individuals, deemed to be too close to the aristocracy or in other ways enemies of the Revolution, were executed across France in the space of about a year.

In hindsight, we can see that the French Revolution was alarming even before it turned so bloodthirsty, for the simple reason that it was so sweeping. Everything was to be subordinated to politics. The names of the months were to be replaced with seasonal names instead of the ones suggestive of pagan gods. Churches were repurposed as temples to "reason." Titles were eliminated and large estates confiscated. Troops were raised to march on surrounding monarchical nations in order to spread the revolution around the globe, setting the stage for Napoleon's conquests as he brought a semblance of order to the chaos and infighting of the Revolution.

All the while, the French revolutionaries swore they were creating a better world. Back in the fledgling United States, some American Revolution veterans, including Thomas Jefferson and Tom Paine, agreed with the French to a point, overestimating the French revolt's similarity to our own.

But at heart, our revolution aimed to cut ties to an abusive government while the French revolution aspired to hand government enough power to fix all of society. Both revolutions used "liberty" as a slogan, but the Americans believed in leaving one another alone, while the French dreamed of purging all corrupt or irrational elements of society. The latter dream will always end in a nightmare whether its rationale is leftist, rightist, religious, or secular and whether the dream is sold to the public in liberationist or authoritarian terminology.

Though celebrated to this day, the French Revolution is one of the most important historical lessons about what *not* to do in politics. It doesn't mean we must embrace the authoritarian and arbitrary monarchy that preceded the French Revolution and inspired it—just as the flaws in our own political system don't mean we should bring back King George III. But it should give zealous political partisans of all stripes pause. People who think they have the right to impose their grand political design on the entire populace tend to discover that large portions of the populace must be gotten rid of lest they become obstacles.

Fortunately, the United States has seen less of the sort of zeal that turned France into a bloodbath for a generation. Instead, what we have had to contend with is the slow, steady—almost boring—erosion of liberty through the gradual accumulation of new laws, new regulations, new taxes, and new reasons for surveillance of the populace.

Responsible Individuals, Responsible Government

Just over a year after the 2014 election that sent me to Washington, Congress once more faced an immense, last-minute omnibus spending bill. We passed the $1.1 trillion monster in the final days of 2015 out of fear that the government would shut down in 2016 if we didn't. Virtually no one had time to read it. It was filled with surprises, including gifts to Obama such as aid to and relocation funds for immigrants, the sort of thing we thought we wouldn't have to fight over again during Obama's presidency, as well as the Cybersecurity Information Sharing Act (CISA) bill, which provided expanded cybersnooping on innocent Americans and which had previously been defeated.

A spending bill of this size ends up touching on everything from poverty programs to military spending and offering goodies to almost every member of Congress to increase the odds that they'll vote for the whole thing rather than pick it apart and risk their pet projects being abandoned. Whereas the Founders strictly enumerated the powers and functions of the federal government and looked with skepticism upon its every expansion, 228 years after the ratification of the Constitution our default method of governing is to fund whatever we funded last year, sometimes at much higher levels, and hope the whole absurd, unexamined can of programs and subsidies can be ignored another year without catastrophe. The crisis of indecision and buck passing is permanent.

Surely, the men who saw King George III as an unacceptable, intrusive threat would have thought no more highly of the mountain of regulations and expenditures under which we now labor. The Declaration of Independence condemned him for, among other things, creating "a multitude of new offices [and sending] hither swarms of officers to harass our people and eat out their substance."

Many Americans might now welcome the relatively small and modest colonial governments of King George's reign, but the hope of the American revolutionaries was to forge a government that would remain small and be more bound by predictable law than King George's agents had been.

The advantages of a small government like the one the Founders envisioned were not imagined to be solely economic.

Their belief in the benefits of rational self-interest was compatible with their everyday experiences in the colonies, the mercantile attitudes of their English forebears, laissez-faire-leaning philosophers such as Locke, and the Puritan work ethic. But complementing that impulse—and sometimes at odds with it—was the Founders' belief in republican virtue. By that I don't mean the precise agenda of today's Republican Party, though my party and before it Jefferson's Democratic-Republican Party both get their name from the concept. Rather, republican virtue harkened back to the Greek city-states and the idea of Roman honor (at least as far as those things were understood centuries later by Colonial Americans).

For a society to be largely self-regulating instead of continually controlled by monarchs and magistrates, its individual members need to possess good character—moral self-discipline—and some sense of civic engagement. The idea of civic engagement—that ordinary citizens should participate in governance—has sometimes been abused by those who wish to subordinate all of life to the political impulse. Rousseau abused the idea when he openly dreamed of turning eighteenth-century Paris into a society modeled on Sparta, all ranks and orders and the suppression of individual will. But if treated as a *complement* to individual freedom instead of a substitute for it, republican virtue can keep a society from handing over all political responsibility to a detached elite.

I emphasized the connection between individual virtue and a responsible approach to political economy in my long-shot primary campaign. Citizens should not have to keep track of $4 trillion worth of annual federal spending. Nor should the economy depend upon the vain hope that a huge lump sum will be spent wisely by a few hundred politicians who never had to work to earn it and can just seize more next year. But the individual citizen can exercise civic virtue simply by not too readily accepting the shifting of the responsibility for all that spending.

We are sold on the idea of letting Washington call the shots by rhetoric that frames DC as a locus of hope, change, progress, moral responsibility, and compassion. Any politician who has spent time there and keeps talking about the place in those terms is lying to you, and that's wrong. Even my own party's theorists have lately created language about how the "federal government works for *you!*" The Founders would roll over. State and local government can work for you, if you say so, but I don't think most folks want the federal government working for them. It would be closer to the truth to say that the capital—meant by the Founders to be the center of a bold new experiment in liberty—has become the place where talented grifters make connections both in government and the private sector, would-be social engineers gain power over their fellow human beings, and your money vanishes down a deep hole.

Far from being a source of moral guidance, Washington insiders strive to get away with a great deal without the public noticing or becoming outraged. Upon examination, their public defenses of what they do—"investments in the future," "making sure we're all paying our fair share," "providing essential infrastructure"—tend to be barely plausible salves to their own consciences and handy public relations buzzwords for keeping the press and the general populace at bay.

The impulse to remake the world with political edicts is hardly limited to Washington, of course. Michael Bloomberg, a former mayor of New York City, is just one of countless political figures who supports authoritarian, intrusive positions on a wide variety of petty issues, from the size of sugary beverages served in a movie theater to the number of cars permitted in a modern city center. Not to mention his dreams of eliminating handguns and global warming gases. States and localities across the nation burden Americans with complex regulations, determining the appearance of private homes, deciding who can run a licensed business, micromanaging land use. Regulators aren't beheading people with a guillotine, but they are a constant nuisance, raising the cost of doing business, which means higher prices for products, and undermining profits, making businesses less likely to expand and hire new people, the last thing an underemployed America needs.

Under the Constitution, Congress should let states and localities make their own rules, but Congress can't stop tilting the playing field in the direction of ever more regulation. Instead, Washington foists unfunded mandates on states and often threatens to withhold federal funds from states that do not impose regulations to the federal government's liking—funds paid for by those states' own citizens through taxes. With one hand, the feds take away, and with the other they give a little back. If you are willing to obey.

Term Limits Can Keep Legislators in Touch with Reality

At the end of 2015, the Federal Register, the official list of regulations, had grown to more than 81,600 pages.[5] Each boring bit of ink on those pages is an edict that the government will enforce against you with fines and, if it comes down to it, jail time (not that I'm recommending you get into a violent standoff). If more members of Congress are elected who think, as I do, that we should be repealing or at least reviewing virtually all regulations, not creating new ones, we can at least set a new tone for the nation, help create a model where citizens are once more trusted to shape their own destinies and solve their own problems rather than be molded by government.

One change in the law, attempted twenty years ago but struck down by the Supreme Court, that might have helped close the gap between the high-and-mighty plans of the politicians is term limits. The turnover rate in Congress is very low. In the 2012 elections, 91 percent of Congress was reelected at the same time that Congress had a 10 percent approval rating from the public.[6] Some progovernment commentators react to this apparent contradiction by arguing that people must not really dislike their legislators as much as they say they do. They contend that the public are just hypocrites, like people who want more and more government spending but do not want to pay more taxes.

I think there's another explanation. Similar to many other aspects of government, electing legislators is a bit like what we call in economics a "prisoner's dilemma." The term is inspired by situations in which two prisoners, being interrogated separately, would fare best if both kept their mouths shut. But each is reminded by the interrogators that it's better to be the one who talks first, so you can make a deal with the captors before your companion does. That's an ugly position to be in, but many Americans view their local elected representative the same way. It'd be nice to throw *all* the bums out, but if that's not going to happen, voters want to keep their own representative, who may by now have seniority, prestige, and success in bringing pork back to the district.

I faced that attitude time and again during my own 2014 campaign when voters told me they shared my positions but feared our district would have less pull if they put a newcomer into Congress. Politics, especially politics in a system where you have to be in the majority to get anything done, easily breeds the attitude that winning is all (or nearly all) that matters. So much effort is put into advertising, fund-raising, messaging, rallying supporters, and undermining the other party that after election day voters are almost too exhausted to ask the depressing question: Did "our" winner end up doing any of the things he promised?

Term limits at least give us new blood. The longer legislators are in office, the more connections they develop—both inside government and in powerful lobbying industries—the more detached they become from the desires of constituents, and the more normal and natural the bubble of DC seems. It could happen to me or even to you if you were elected to a legislature. Republican presidential contender Marco Rubio, generally agreed to be a solidly "establishment" figure, even went so far in late 2015 as to recommend a constitutional convention to create a term-limiting amendment that would pass muster with the Supreme Court. Risky but perhaps useful.

The Constitution specifies that congressional terms be determined at the federal level, so the 1990s effort to impose term limits state by state, though highly popular, was eventually deemed unconstitutional. Not surprisingly, the subsequent effort to get legislators to limit their terms *voluntarily* hasn't gotten great results. No politician wants to be the first one to head to the exit door. And sometimes a particularly ambitious politician has no respect for tradition and precedent alone if it's not codified in law, as when Franklin Delano Roosevelt ignored the two-terms-and-out tradition that had been established by the first president, George Washington, and had held for a century and a half thereafter. FDR's contempt for precedent, the Supreme Court, and rule of law (making him something of a revolutionary at heart but not the good kind) quickly inspired an amendment officially limiting presidents to two terms, but no such limit has yet been imposed on Congress.

I will fight for term limits in Congress, though as with so many other battles to limit this leviathan, it will be an uphill struggle. But fighting the battle at the federal level has one advantage over fighting it in piecemeal fashion: as the prisoner's dilemma idea teaches us, people can achieve bigger rewards when they understand that everyone will accept restrictions *simultaneously*. Assure legislators that they will not be shooting themselves in the foot while their rivals go on to long, illustrious legislative careers, and they may be willing to restore the high-turnover "citizen legislature" the Founders envisioned.

That has implications for the regulatory regime we exist under, too. Nothing inspires caution and thoughtfulness in the crafting of legislation like knowing you'll soon be living under the very rules you have made. Congress routinely exempts itself from the regulations it creates—including Obamacare participation rules and rules against your relatives trading stocks based on inside knowledge of anticipated legislation—though twenty years ago there was a noble effort by Speaker Newt Gingrich to end the practice.

Few things better illustrate Congress's unhealthy esteem for itself than its assumption that laws are for other, lesser people, the kinds of people who don't spend decades occupying seats in Congress.

The Spirit of '76 Helps Us Still

For all the flaws in the system we've inherited, our republic has this much going for it: it offers the hope of change without violent revolution. Though Thomas Jefferson dreamed, a bit fanatically, of the American Revolution being periodically renewed through the shedding of blood, it's still possible for us to do something much more mature and morally impressive: we can end our government's abuses and correct its excesses through the legal traditions we have inherited and by remembering the *moral* traditions we have inherited alongside them.

People on the right and left alike sense that the nation is in a time of crisis. The difference is that the left is always ready to abandon everything that worked in the past for the latest pleasant-sounding remedy. The economy falters in large part because of big government, and Bernie Sanders suggests giving democratic socialism a try. Hillary Clinton sounds a bit more moderate—her bad ideas are more along the lines of hiking the capital gains tax—but still declares that capitalism "needs to be reinvented."[7] The left loves the idea of a break with America's purportedly tainted past.

By contrast, conservatives, libertarians, and a growing number of moderates suspect the solutions to our problems lie in the past that the left denigrates. America does not need a revolution that *reverses* its founding principles; it needs to recover those founding principles and see history as proof that they work. The American Revolution already happened, and it was a great success.

Consider, if you will, how radical the Revolution was. States have grown and shrunk throughout history, but at the time the American Revolution occurred it was recognized around the world as the first case of a people consciously writing the ground rules for their society and doing so along rational lines conducive to the general welfare. In the process, the Revolution eliminated both aristocracy and monarchy, a social upheaval bigger than anything Bernie Sanders's supporters typically envision.

Yes, there was far more work to be done. Rights initially possessed only by free non–Native American males had to be extended over the next two centuries to blacks, women, and Native Americans. But the Revolution provided the *formula* for setting the whole world free, not just a small, self-serving fraction, as the far left sometimes likes to portray it. The formula blended the best of the English legal tradition's individualism with the new eighteenth-century optimism about the possibility of rendering law simple, clear, and rational. It did for justice something similar to what Isaac Newton had done for physics one century earlier by deducing the basic laws of gravitation. In neither case can the whole story be told in one short sentence, but in both cases, we can spot many of the alternative theories as flawed, even crackpot, substitutes.

Like Newton's laws, the principles of the American Revolution work because they are not arbitrary. They are not "relative" to one time and place. They are timeless, though humanity is in the long, gradual process of learning about them. In other words, since the dawn of history it has been true that limiting government's ability to interfere with the plans of ordinary citizens—and legally forbidding those citizens to attack one another—while protecting against invasions from outside has been a sensible formula for a society's success. But sometimes people must try numerous wrong ways before they are confident that they've seen proof that sensible alternatives can work.

The American Revolutionaries, particularly Jefferson in the Declaration of Independence, proclaimed the new nation with the confidence, perhaps unique to their era, of rationalist philosophers who had deduced the correct answer to humanity's social problems. And I think they had. However, just as Newton said he stood upon "the shoulders of giants" in deriving his gravitational formulas, the Founders looked to the past—particularly classical antiquity, with the philosophical and legal models provided by Greece and Rome—both for intellectual models and historical evidence about what political models endure. By severing their ties to the Old World, they were taking one of the biggest political risks in history, perhaps the most important of all time.

They were painfully conscious of the fact that they would be judged not only by God and posterity but by their contemporaries around the world, who were waiting to see if this "new republic" was a fantasy or the shape of political things to come. Their future—now over two centuries of our past—would either refute their beliefs in individualism, rights, commerce, and limited government or provide the best experimental evidence for these beliefs the world had yet seen.

I think the Revolution and the subsequent experiment that is US history have already proven successful.

Our failures have come not from being duped by the Founders into holding the wrong beliefs but from straying time and again from the path they set us on. The temptation to stray is recurring and powerful. Americans felt it even during the Revolution, with talk of making George Washington a new king. They felt the pull toward seemingly easier, authoritarian solutions in the form of Confederate rationales for slavery, Progressive arguments for abandoning laissez-faire capitalism, FDR's arguments for big government, the poverty-based arguments for a massive welfare state, the pseudocapitalist arguments for subsidies to businesses and banks, and recently race- and sex-based arguments for ever more regulations.

Consider the daring of the American revolutionaries. They had pronounced their intention to tame government and live as free people long before they had the numerous examples of what government can do at its worst. They hadn't seen the poverty and starvation caused by the communist revolutions in Russia and China. They hadn't seen the Nazis' Holocaust. They hadn't seen the gleaming skyscrapers of modern American cities or the United States wielding influence around the globe. They hadn't seen two centuries of American inventions, entertainment, population growth, and prosperity. For the most part, they had only seen farming and the various industries necessary to keep a population of farmers alive, from tanning to wagon construction and shipping.

But in a sense they knew what was possible on this continent better than some of our contemporaries do. Their confidence in those principles made all that followed happen, and all that followed has been their vindication, their proof.

That Revolution Didn't Come Out of Nowhere

Revolutionaries though they may have been, they weren't just flying blind, and they didn't deduce their political principles solely from watching blacksmiths and tradesmen at work. However, there is a great deal to be learned from watching the economy function. (We'll revisit that topic in detail in Chapter 12.) The American Revolutionaries, like many eighteenth-century intellectuals, were self-consciously neo-classical in their thinking. That is, they hoped to recapture some of the philosophical grandeur of Greece and Rome to which all of Western civilization was indebted.

That in itself shows the revolutionaries balanced tendencies we now associate with the right and the left, and it's perhaps the reason both sides sometimes try to claim the mantle of the American Revolution. In truth, our modern conception of right-wing and left-wing political factions had barely arisen then. What did exist, and in some ways resembles today's political spectrum, was the tension between following in the footsteps of one's predecessors and improving things by deploying new ideas. That debate—described by the French in the late seventeenth century as a "quarrel between the ancients and the moderns"—captured the era's anxiety. New things were afoot, but would they lead to greatness or ruin?

If thinkers of the day could prove they were still adhering to the wisdom of glorious past eras while solving practical political problems, they could assure the world that they were not acting without precedent. An experiment was under way, but it was in accord with the most esteemed lessons from a shared past.

For all practical purposes, that cultural past begins with ancient Greek philosophy. If we are next to wrestle with the Greeks, we must wrestle with the philosopher Plato. No wonder the left has reacted so furiously on campus in recent decades against the conservatives who suggest beginning modern education there. As I shall explain in the next chapter, the left has little interest in teaching Plato because it has little interest in teaching ethics in general. I'll also explain how that came to pass with some editorial assistance from a political writer friend of mine. Much of Western history was lost in the attempt to erase the influence of the Judeo-Christian tradition. As a Calvinist very much rooted in the tradition, married to a Catholic, I find that effort to erase history alarming.

chapter six

PLATO: IDEAL SCENARIOS

Amidst all the conflicting perspectives in American politics, you still hear the occasional plea for objective standards—moral and legal rules that lift us above the conflict to survey how absurd things are and how much better they could be. The search for a higher standard is as old as Western civilization, and it may help put many things into perspective if we see how it began with ancient Greek philosophers and spread into the world we know.

It is no secret that many politicians change their views, sometimes even reverse them, to suit their current audience. Countless candidates are for budget cuts until it affects their own districts, deregulation until it upsets a major donor, reform until it causes a frenzy in the press. Generally speaking, politicians are not philosophers. If they were, according to the ancient Greeks, they would have views based on a much more solid foundation than shifting polls. They might be happier people, standing firm instead of endlessly twisting to capture a few more votes. In Plato's terms, they would be turning their attention away from flickering shadows on a cave wall toward the permanence of the Forms, the fire at the heart of the cave.

While searching modern Washington, DC, for signs of the "republican virtue" the Founders admired, it is tempting to conclude that there is no virtue of any kind. Making connections is more important than making friends, accumulating power more important than sticking to principles. The moral decline contributes to our potential national decline. Ethics is in short supply.

For the serious-minded people interested in this topic, I refer you to the school of philosophy called logical positivism created by the brightest minds in the world about a hundred years ago. They tried at long last to produce a philosophy that was both logical and a "positive" source of knowledge for all claims. It failed. But the great Bertrand Russell, Rudolf Carnap, and Ludwig Wittgenstein had the character to admit that it failed. Since then, academic philosophy has not produced a serious ethics of note. Not one. So though Nietzsche said, "God is dead,"[1] in actuality, academic ethics is dead!

For a more practical view of what has gone wrong in our modern world of ideas, let's start by examining the typical MBA textbook on business ethics. I always refer to a standard text used at the University of Virginia and written by one of its senior professors. It has fifty pages of ethics, then four hundred pages of case studies. So the fifty pages on ethics had better be pretty good. It is good, in a way. This book, like any other used in academic ethics, will always, and I mean always, refer to three major schools of thought in ethics. They are: the Kantians, the utilitarians, and then Aristotle's ethics, which is sometimes called Virtue Theory in business, developed out of the same Greek milieu as Plato.

These are all excellent systematic accounts of ethics. Kant is arguably the most important philosopher and ethicist of the modern world. Aristotle was one of the most significant philosophers and ethicists of the ancient world, but he also has a major hold on the modern world as his system largely informs the Catholic tradition. And we are all utilitarians at a practical level. Should we build a school or a new bridge? The utilitarian answer would be the one that brings the greatest happiness to the greatest number of folks.

Though they're substantial ethical schools of thought, they all suffer from one major flaw: they don't have any followers. That is a problem. I usually ask my audience if they meet many Kantians or utilitarians when they go out for beers or tea. They laugh. Then I ask if they have friends that are Jewish, Christian, Muslim, Buddhist, or Confucian, and every hand goes up. Vast majorities of real people around the globe live out these religious traditions, but for some reason, we teach academic ethics, which is good for critical thinking, instead of the ethics that people actually live.

That issue is touched on in George Marsden's book *The Soul of the American University: From Protestant Establishment to Established Nonbelief.* According to Marsden, it is well known that most of the colleges and universities founded in the United States before the twentieth century had a strongly religious, usually Protestant Christian, character and that virtually all those institutions have no significant religious identity today. (My goal here is not to overly lament the loss of this Protestant culture but to show the symbolic deal that was struck and the implications it had for the future course of ethics.)

The best-known example is Harvard, founded "for the provision of a learned ministry," whose motto for three centuries was "Veritas Christo et Ecclesiae" (Truth for Christ and Church). But scores of other institutions, including Yale, Princeton, Chicago, Stanford, Duke, and Boston University, and even publicly funded state universities such as Michigan and California, had a pronounced Christian character in the early years of their existence and abandoned it in the twentieth century. Think of that. Harvard: Truth for Christ and Church for three hundred years, until about 1900; now reason and religion are both under assault there. What happened? Marsden's overall thesis is that the leading figures in those institutions subscribed to the agenda of creating a national, nonsectarian Protestant public culture.

In sum, he argues that the Protestant institutions made a gentleman's agreement with the broader culture: we Protestants will hand over the universities to the culture if you will teach the basic ethical canon of Western culture. You do not need to teach the Christian faith, but we know that you cannot teach the canon without bumping into this tradition. The handshake occurred. Universities transferred power to new boards, and new curricula emerged. Seminaries moved across the tracks. But the broader culture told a whopper! They did not maintain ethics in education. At present there are no required ethics classes, and mandatory history courses are rare as well.

Marsden outlines the move toward the creation of this national, sectarian, Protestant public culture. He notes that the Protestants actually succeeded in terms of the national public culture, which was distinctively Protestant until World War II, but in the process the religious identity of their colleges and universities disappeared because nonsectarian Protestantism had little or no content that could withstand the challenges from empirical science and the demand to accommodate an increasing pluralism of beliefs, including nonbelief.

One of the most poignant claims Marsden makes is that the leaders of the American Protestant universities did not intend the secularization their institutions underwent. Indeed, they insisted that the changes for particular short-term benefits would actually strengthen the Christian character of their institutions. They seem not to have understood the forces they were yielding to. Their conception of religion led them to identify with the mainstream culture rather than offer a prophetic criticism of it. In the end, the institutions did not have an intellectual theology or a view of education healthy enough to engage the powerful influences of modernity on equal terms.

During the half century from about 1870 to 1920, the faith that had founded and structured the universities would be routinely ignored, pilloried, and rejected. Marsden finds a key to this process in the bombshell of a book William F. Buckley, Jr., published in 1951 called *God and Man at Yale*. Reviewing his texts and teachers at Yale, Buckley pointed to "the triumph of 'relativism, pragmatism, and utilitarianism'" in the spirit of the philosopher John Dewey. "There is surely not a department at Yale," Buckley observed, "that is uncontaminated with the absolute that there are no absolutes, no intrinsic rights, no ultimate truths."

Generally speaking, by the end of the nineteenth century, colleges such as Harvard retained a commitment to only a vaguely Christian morality. For example, Harvard's president Charles Eliot Norton announced, "The moral purpose of a university's policy should be to train young men to self-control and self-reliance through liberty."[2] I always get a kick out of that one. Training young men to *discipline through liberty*? Optimistic visions of human nature were in the air. The Western canon had few writers who could testify to a good human nature. Actually, most knew that human nature was far from what it could be. Rousseau was the stark exception. He was a consistent liberal, seeing human nature as inherently good and so in no need of moral education. It was good and consistent thinking but wrong in the end.

Committed to the notion of human goodness, Harvard's Norton embraced William James's voluntarism, defining man's nature as the result of exercising his free will. So he eliminated required courses (Latin, Greek, and the classics, including doses of Bible and Christian theology) in favor of electives, allowing students to design their own course of studies.

Today, this trend has escalated to the point where there are no required courses in ethics or religion or philosophy across the leading schools in our country. Ethics is gone. Optimistic assumptions about human nature remain in higher education even after Hitler lived and died—and, more important, with no definition of the good. It is far easier to claim that one is good if there is no definition of or criterion for the good, I suppose. There is no bar to clear. We are all good. Did I note that we do well on self-esteem tests? If we put God into the equation and compare ourselves to that standard, though, we will likely get a far different assessment of our goodness.

Can a free society or economy stand with this vague moral foundation? The evidence does not look promising. Common sense tells us that we should simply get back to ethics. But after a quick history lesson on ethics, I think it will become clear why we will not return to it. In short, the whole tradition is built upon two structural foundations: the Judeo-Christian tradition and (after the Greek model) human reason. The entire language, art, and culture of the West are built on this dual foundation. To return to ethics is to return to those structures. Many in academia, especially on the left, do not want anything to do with them. Some think they are responsible for human misery and the negative beliefs making up the modern left's ethical vocabulary: sexism, chauvinism, prejudice, homophobia, racism, patriarchy, hegemony, xenophobia, bigotry, bias, discrimination, colonialism, capitalism, exploitation, subjugation, interventionism, and so on.

If traditional ethics leads to that, the left doesn't want tradition or ethics. What does it want? It cannot say. It has no philosophy in mind at all.

Ancient Moral Roots and Modern Political Fruit

But what was ethics while it lasted? To grasp that, we must look back at the earliest building blocks of the Judeo-Christian ethos, not merely because it is "our" ethos but because it *worked* and eventually bequeathed us the greatest successes of the modern world. We should also look even earlier, to the Greco-Roman world.

In the Jewish and Christian histories, moral freedom would often be referred to as freedom of conscience, particularly as those traditions matured. The concept is, of course, part of mainstream language today. We all deeply resent coercion in this realm. The view is widely shared, and it's one of the major points of this book. The tradition and its moral foundations are the foundations of the modern world.

In about 1400, the concepts of "freedom of conscience" and "toleration" would become even more substantial. They were so respected that people would eventually demand that they become "rights." These rights are "claims" that must be respected. They cannot be optional. Hitler cannot claim an exceptional case. The UN declares rights to be universal. They apply to all people at all times. In the US revolution, the people became sovereign, not the king. The rights were zealously protected by law. The First Amendment to the Constitution protects our freedom of religion and expression. This impulse flowed directly from freedom of conscience and noncoercion.

Early modernity, about seven hundred years ago, was a pivotal time when adherents of Judaism, Christianity, and Islam could all still talk to one another in the common language of Greek philosophy (despite the Crusades). In 1300, Christians, Jews, and Muslims shared the common ethics of Aristotle. They shared a language and even agreed on many of the deep assumptions embedded in those ethics. Since then, they have drifted apart, Islam arguably frozen by its antisecular religiosity. Bernard Lewis is right when he says that we now face a clash of civilizations between Islam and the West.[3] But it needn't have turned out like this, not if everyone had remembered the example of dialogue set earlier by a shared heritage of respect for the Greek philosophers.

Though Rousseau's ethos was dangerous, as discussed in the previous chapter, even his thought had its roots in the ancient world. Fortunately, Athens, one of the Greek city-states, developed democratic ideals that would foster a Western political tradition larger than Rousseau.

A Thank-you to the Greeks

I admit that ancient Athens looks authoritarian and alien to our modern eyes. There were slaves, frequent wars, subjugated women, and political assassinations. But Athens was also the cradle of the idea that each citizen was the potential moral equal of any other, with each having a role to play in governance. In theory, each Athenian mattered and not just as a member of a military phalanx.

Those subtly individualistic political and philosophical traditions would be echoed in Rome and even shape the thinking in the New Testament. I would not want for a moment to dismiss the indebtedness of Christianity to Judaism or even direct revelation, but the timeless moral battles fought therein clearly take place in a Roman-ruled society that feels a bit more familiar to us than the bloodier tribal warrior cultures that preceded Greece and Rome. Jesus's world was one of lawyers and philosophers, not just warriors. If it had been made up of only warriors, He might have received an even harsher reception than He did. Plato and the Greek philosophical tradition are owed some thanks for the relative civility of the Roman world.

To understand Plato, we must in turn consider his mentor Socrates, known to us mainly through his dialogues with students, recounted by Plato in the fourth century BC.

Socrates saw that properly understood reason is not a unifier or a cement that keeps the status quo in place. Though in the end he submitted willingly to the laws of Athens, drinking poison as his death sentence for questioning the gods, he was definitely not just an obedient adherent to the customs of his society. He followed his community's laws, but he did not think any claim beyond skeptical inquiry was above questioning. It may sound odd for a conservative to say this, but Socrates was arguably the most important philosopher in the entire Western tradition precisely because he was a subversive.

He did not subvert merely for the sake of causing chaos, either. Like his student Plato, he believed there was a good to be found through inquiry. Socrates continually asked his students to reexamine their premises but did not expect only emptiness to result. He expected, gradually and imperfectly, to discover what truly matters. Yet his quest sufficiently unsettled the rulers of Athens, and they sentenced him to death because they believed he was corrupting the minds of the young. We now recognize those questioning minds not as victims but as the first real participants in the dialogue that forms the story of Western civilization.

Much like Christian thinkers but half a millennium earlier, Socrates valued the individual's internal struggle to find his way toward the good—without saying "anything goes" or merely turning the responsibility for decision making over to authoritarian rulers. There is an internal moral sense, attuned to the moral structure of the larger universe, and it can be understood by reason.

In much the way Christianity undermined the fatalism of rival creeds by prioritizing the struggle of the individual conscience, Socrates's methodical inquiries were an alternative to the resigned attitude of the stoics and the ancient tendency to see natural law as something decreeing a world that was predictable, hierarchical, but without hope. There was a whiff of freedom in Socrates's thinking.

Plato was more of a system builder than Socrates. As would happen on so many subsequent occasions in the history of Western thought, a teacher arrived in part to tear down and his pupil to build anew. Plato reminded us that reason should "aim higher" than everyday concerns and examine *ideals*, not be reduced to mere instrumental rationality (such as the loveless and cynical big government of Rome). By daring to ask what an ideal republic would look like, Plato did an immense service to all subsequent political thinkers. Like Socrates, he boldly engaged in imagining a culture beyond inherited, traditional rules at a time when few human beings had ever known anything but unquestioning obedience to the traditions of village and city.

Socrates and Plato are the great-great-grandparents, so to speak, of thinkers such as Locke, who believed the fallen political constructs of humanity could be judged by a higher moral order. It has been said that all Western philosophy is ultimately a footnote to Plato.

Plato Aims Higher

Plato recognized that most people either obey laws out of habit and custom or view all morals as a fiction, "relative" to a given person's preferences, as the pre-Socratic philosopher Protagoras did. Few people recognize that man-made laws, though better than lawlessness, are but a crude approximation of the good, toward which philosophers must continue to strive and, when given the chance to influence public affairs, toward which they can sometimes nudge whole societies.

If the laws and beliefs of most people are only an approximation of the good, argued Plato in a famous metaphor, those ideas are a little like shadows cast upon a cave wall. Then philosophy is the rare act of turning one's gaze from the cave wall toward the fire at the center of the cave.

Across the Mediterranean, the light at the center of all things might by then have been called Yahweh and worshipped to the exclusion of other, older gods. Plato's culture was still polytheistic, but the Greek philosophers spoke with surprising frequency of a God higher and more abstract than the characters of myth such as Zeus. Those traditions, rooted in Athens and Jerusalem, would meet prominently five centuries later—and in our next chapter. But the fire at the center of the cave is not quite as specific as God (or gods). It is, we might abstractly say, the light of truth.

Just as in principle the light of truth was accessible to all, so was the divine law being promulgated by Moses. This pattern of turning from the particular to the universal would recur throughout Western history and lead to some of its grandest insights.

What Plato discerned at the metaphorical heart of the cave, by turning away from the shadow-puppet-like display on its walls, might also be called *the natural law*, in contrast to incidental—yet highly necessary—man-made laws. Think of it as a genuine discovery akin to the investigation of scientific and economic laws that would take place more than two millennia later, in the era of the US Founders. Much as scientists and economists recognize the difference between ideal cases—models of how the universe would work absent complicating details—Plato argued that there are ideal Forms of any given object in the material world beyond the sensory one.

Plato also saw the dichotomy between what reason and human rulers demanded in politics, but he was aware of what had become of his mentor Socrates for pointing out such a distinction. Plato would have to be more politic. He would have to speak to some degree in veiled language, a bit like Jesus speaking in parables to his followers centuries later. In written dialogues using a fictionalized Socrates as a mouthpiece for Plato's own political views, Plato described an ideal Republic, one noticeably at odds with the real Athenian democracy he lived in. He portrayed a society divided into three classes of humans: workers, guardians, and rulers, who, tellingly, would ideally be "philosopher kings."

Yet Plato could not have been so presumptuous to think this sketch would lead to him being declared ruler of Athens, and it would have been dangerous for him to imply that. Think of his Republic, then, partly as a model for the philosophizing mind itself, setting reason at the pinnacle, moral courage just below, and the ordinary functions of life lower still. Still, as with the concept of "republican virtue" discussed earlier, this was the start of the idea that model citizens—who are in some sense *self*-governing because they are guided by morals and reason—are the foundation that makes moral societies and politics possible. Then as now, we neglect that foundation at our peril.

Then as now, we see the need for philosophers to address higher, more long-term philosophical battles than the messy personal fights of the moment and sometimes to write or speak in a partly veiled fashion.

The whole world is watching, and one wrong word can set off a controversy these days, yet serious-minded people engaged in the battle of ideas must still be able to address each other. Careless attention seekers talk as if only the next election or financial quarter matters. But thoughtful people know that the real issues facing our republic span centuries and deserve careful reflection, ruminations engaged in without fear of government censors or politically correct bullies. Since the thugs often can't be shouted down, sometimes the best strategy is to speak in the quiet tones of academia or even theology while the noisy crowd passes by without noticing, sometimes without realizing how badly it needs those quieter voices to reach true conclusions and implement wise policies.

Politics Aims Lower

The Greeks respected the art of rhetoric because they were accustomed to a democracy in which reason functioned largely through dialogue, such as that between teachers and pupils, and arguments were presented before the Athenian assembly. Setting another example that would be noted by our own Founders over two thousand years later, the Greeks were also conscious of the contrast between an orator and a demagogue. A speaker can state his case by appealing first to common ground without abandoning all principle and simply saying whatever will sway the crowd.

Compare the Greeks' cautious, moral approach to the current state of US politics. In an environment where grabbing public attention is the necessary first step to getting funding and votes, many politicians, as the saying goes, will say anything to get elected. Say something outrageous—the more irrational the better, it often seems—and far from being batted down by a modern-day Socrates, you may well be rewarded with extra media attention: TV appearances, Facebook likes, tweets. You don't even need honeyed words anymore, since getting people angry, confused, or generally stirred up may generate just as much attention. Politics gets reduced to some very hasty aesthetic judgments.

Plato foresaw this. To the average philosophy student today, it sounds bizarre that Plato suggested banning poets from his ideal Republic. It makes him seem like a cranky, perhaps overly conservative, censor who hated flowery words. But if, once more, we do not take his admonition literally but instead consider what he was telling us about human reason, we see the sense in his prohibition. He was warning that poets—like many other types of artists and today more than a few online BS artists—can appeal to our passions instead of our reason and lead the republic astray in its political judgments.

If someone living in our era gets his passionate snap political judgments from a movie he's seen or a rock band he loves, what is he doing if not substituting poetry for more considered political judgment? It was dangerous in Plato's day, and it's dangerous in ours, though literal censorship is not the answer. The answer is to cultivate our rational faculties and our skepticism so we can spot the lies and the double-talk. I tried to take that approach in my primary campaign by citing numbers about the debt and asking people to look at the contrast in Washington between rhetoric and legislative record.

The appeal to reason worked. By contrast, in a battle of aesthetics, who knows what may happen and who will win out?

No Politics without Ethics

Part of the appeal of fascism and communism in the twentieth century was obviously their romanticism, the broad aesthetic strokes suggested by Nazi bonfires and red communist flags over barricades, not any serious mastery of details of genetics, economics, or history. Nazi pseudoscience really was the sort of thing a poet might cook up, with fairy-tale appeals to medieval and tribal imagery. Karl Marx's economic ideas, still treated with respect by all too many of my fellow professors, were shot through with metaphors about werewolves and vampires, to which he likened the evil capitalist exploiter class.

But Marx, whom we'll revisit later, never raises two questions that are crucial for his own ethical doctrine. First, what principles or criteria are to inform the working-class movement? Marx gives us no ethics, no rules, and no constitution. In effect, he just says, "Trust me." Capitalism would force confrontation between owners of capital and workers, but how does the transition from capitalism to socialism take place? Second, how does Marx conceive it possible that a society prone to the errors of moral individualism may come to recognize and transcend them? The bad guys are bad in his cosmology because they are capitalists and self-interested. So replace the capitalist leaders with communist leaders, and they will not be self-interested and will care only about the good. Well, how can that be? Of course, Marx would say that the material conditions of communism would change human behavior. Once the members of the brotherhood are all made equal, then the good will emerge!

If ethics is about the criteria for what is good, Marx does not have ethics. He does have a revolutionary charge against injustice as he sees it, but a revolutionary charge without ethics should cause concern. The American Revolution was founded on the Western synthesis of religion and reason. The American Founders were not utopian. They held a Calvinist/Puritan attitude toward human nature: that nature is not good. That is why they sought to divide power at every turn, because reason and history told them that rulers will always tend to corruption. They put their hope on the gradual emergence of individual rights that were given by the God of Nature and would now have to find their way into history.

As we saw above, Marx would never produce an ethics for the working class. He simply solved the social problem by declaring all capitalists exploiters. They must go. Central planners would take their place. Central planning would replace the price system. Everyone would get some food, but they would also get the same pair of blue jeans. And they would not get free press or political liberty. The hope for a better day trumps ethics. That is a very dangerous gamble, and so far billions of people have lost on it. Do you want to try your luck?

But this stuff sells, ironically. Ideas like it sold to the masses even two and a half thousand years ago. But they're not the truth. The desire to find the truth must come first, the details of economics and policy later. To place a policy or, worse, a revolutionary goal, prior to the quest for truth is to invite opportunism, whim, and disaster on a grand scale.

Citizen, Govern Thyself

Plato, for all his errors as he navigated through the earliest, crudest version of the maze of Western philosophy, recognized the dangers of letting popular unreason go uncontested. If the mind is like a chariot, he suggested, let it be yoked to reason, not merely to the passions, or you will end up on a very wild ride.

Glance through some political comment threads on Facebook or Twitter these days, and you have to wonder if anyone really cares about keeping politics tethered to sanity. Sentiment can as easily turn to anger and zealotry as to gentleness and compassion. When morals become nothing more than feelings, the eventual result is the belief in nothing more than those feelings: nihilism.

Democracy is a great thing, far superior to dictatorship, but it has its own risks. Almost no politician is ever going to summon the courage to tell an adoring crowd of supporters, "I appreciate your faith in me, but I don't think you've actually thought this through, and you need to learn a lot more about philosophy and economics before deciding on our next policy move."

Like lawyers hoping to pick persuadable people to put on a jury, politicians tend to want supporters who are not totally crazy and yet are not so independent minded and clear thinking as to be immune to the politicians' charms. It is in the interest of the most corrupt politicians to have a populace for whom both morals and political preferences are truly arbitrary, moods to be manipulated through fear, envy, greed, and—this one's effective even among more sophisticated voters—a feeling of urgency.

That is not to say that our society has no philosophers. Even today, centuries later, there are neo-Platonists and neo-Aristotelians, willing to step back and take the long view of the development of Western morals, recognizing how deep and complex our tradition is, rather than jumping on the next political fad. The Canadian philosopher Charles Taylor cautions, though, that Western philosophical history can in some ways be seen as a descent. We've learned things, improved technology and law and in some ways even moral habits, but Western philosophy is always in something of a free fall toward ever-greater individualism, which is both a blessing and a curse.

No matter how many zigs and zags Western philosophy goes through, it keeps returning to the idea that its contradictions can be straightened out with an even larger dose of individualism. We went from tribal life to citizenship within city-states to allegiance to kings and nations that were supposed to respect certain specific rights of at least some citizens to demanding that all members of society be free. Then we went farther still. Over the past century, even as politics continued to revolve around utopian and republican notions that Plato would have recognized, in ethics it seems as though the old foe Protagoras prevailed in the idea that morality is mere subjective whim. Or, as Plato reports Protagoras to have said, "Man is the measure of all things."[4] As old bonds of tradition and morality dissolved, it turned out there was little to prevent the state from filling the resulting vacuum. Ethics was an impediment to political action, as both the fascists and communists knew.

By the nineteenth century, the West's admirable individualism had come tantalizingly close to creating a society without social or political constraints, but intellectuals didn't want that quite as much as they'd imagined. Even as the West grew rich, people recoiled from what was perceived as the chaos and unpredictability of industrial existence. Instead of sticking to a simple law code that protected newly respected individual rights, intellectuals looked to twisted variations on the city-states of old, imagined medieval communities of a harmonious yet noncommercial nature, or wholesale replacement of conventional ethics with social engineering projects (the beginning of "Progressivism").

In each case, the intellectuals reduced personal moral judgment to a secondary role in society. *Planners* would decide what the shape of the world should be. Yet there was no stopping the deeper cultural logic of ever-greater self-expression, ever more "experiments in living," to use John Stuart Mill's phrase.[5]

So a sort of multitiered intellectual model took hold after all, but not one of moral guardians and philosopher kings that Plato had hoped for, nor the private conscience and "rendering unto Caesar" of Christian tradition. The late nineteenth and early twentieth centuries saw the rise of political movements, including fascism and bolshevism but also the subtler rebellion of Nietzsche-influenced bohemians. The adherents of those movements believed that the need for morality had essentially been outgrown because the central planners would decide what must be done, leaving the masses to indulge their passions as long as they obeyed their rulers.

It was a model for an unhealthy paternalism among political elites and a juvenile, irresponsible streak among the ruled. Though primarily a moral and political problem, it also jibed with a rising hedonist streak in the popular culture, the negative side of the (very positive) phenomenon of rising prosperity. If it feels good, do it, as they used to say. Few would put it quite that simply, but the impulsive—and thus unreflective—has an odd tendency to be celebrated by the same people who want regimentation in our laws and regulations. If you create a nearly ungovernable populace, government will have a lot of work to do.

To create a more self-governing populace, you should have an education system that frankly teaches moral reasoning. But campus rebellions have been fighting against that idea for decades now, arguably for a century or more.

There are still people who hew to old-fashioned hopes for moral education in our schools, though. I was at a political event recently, and an elderly lady gave the speaker a good scolding. The speaker was a leading educational expert and held political office. "What about history?" the lady asked. "What are you doing about some real education? These kids are not getting any values in school." The speaker informed her that education could not do everything and that moral education and history needed to take place in the home.

That is a traditional answer, based on the assumption that homes are still moral. After claiming that the family is key, the politician went right into the next talking point and informed the audience that demographics are really shifting at present in the country and more than 50 percent of our kids do not have intact families. Do you see the problem here? Ethical teaching should take place in the family, but the family is broken for over 50 percent of the population. The speaker did not notice the conflict. So in this context, what should education do in order to form good citizens?

I do not mean to suggest that our elite institutions have no memory of our Greek cultural heritage or the moral insights of the ancients. Oddly enough, UNESCO, the United Nations cultural organization, which probably at least imagines itself to play a guardianlike role, declared 2016 an Aristotle Anniversary Year—2,400 years since the philosopher's birth.

Ethics Are Still Relevant, I Hope

Instead of the contemplation of right and wrong, of taking seriously the metaphysical forms beyond this mundane world, the abstractions such as justice and good, we pride ourselves on mastering the pragmatic skills of politicking, lobbying, data mining, and public relations. Having been through political campaigns and House budget battles, not to mention college faculty infighting, I know how much influence all those things can have on our lives. But it's not those things that truly inspire us.

In this ordinary, physical world—this fallen world, we would say in the Christian tradition—the Forms still call to us, philosophy awakens the mind from its number crunching, and there is a historical spine to this civilization that enables it to stand with pride and moral confidence. Though I had the numbers to show voters how badly the economy was doing and how far over budget the federal government was, time and again what appealed to them was the larger moral message that what the government is doing to us *isn't right*. Ethics now seems to trump economics, and this is a good thing.

Talking about morals in the corridors of power sounds naive and elicits snickers even from journalists who are supposed to be keeping the politicians on their best behavior. But the ground rules of a successful civilization, even if discerned from the study of history, must also be written in the human heart. If not, good luck enforcing them. Just watch footage of rioting after sporting events or flash mobs attacking convenience stores to see that police alone can't keep the populace in line if it loses interest in moral behavior altogether.

Still, the Founders understood that "Nature's God," as they put it, had instilled a certain intuitive awareness of moral rules in all thinking people. That would not be possible if those rules were truly arbitrary, only a matter of feeling, whim, and opinion polls. Like Plato before them, the Founders of the United States were in effect detecting the natural law. It calls to us still, and it can survive through the worst of times. It has. At its most basic, it's the rule that says that our respecting all other individuals allows them to flourish even as we wish to flourish. It's a formula for peace and prosperity that unites ethics and economics.

But since the pure abstractions of philosophy easily get forgotten in the hurly-burly of crass normal life—in modern DC as it was in the ancient agora—there must be something a bit more concrete, more grounded in routine customs, to make our highest moral ideals part of the weave of everyday life and everyone's psyche. For Western civilization, that has meant primarily the Judeo-Christian tradition. And now we turn our attention to that crucial thread, but in the context of the slightly more alien ethos of Rome.

chapter seven

DON'T DO EVERYTHING AS THE ROMANS DID

Ｏne of the most frightening results of the reckless growth of government bureaucracy in our day is that it saps our love of country. We love America. We are wearied and made indifferent by its loveless ruling bureaucracy. I want to tell you a similar grim story about ancient Rome, but it has the happiest and most hopeful ending in all of human history, even though the empire does not survive.

Though it is at the very heart of my story—the West's story—invoking our Judeo-Christian heritage raises hackles in some quarters. Law and public policy are meant to apply equally to all citizens, so isn't it unseemly for a politician to mention a specific cultural tradition? Perhaps it is, if one thinks of that tradition in only the narrowest terms, such as on rare occasions to hector one's political enemies. But it's much bigger and older than any one current policy battle. It's our art, our language, our music, our science. It's our history, centuries of ethical and legal development that none of us, secular or religious, could wish away if we wanted to and that we ignore at the price of having a shallower understanding of our institutions.

Sometimes looking back at what preceded the Judeo-Christian tradition can remind us how alien other modes of thought are and how rooted our own most humane, not to mention bipartisan, ethical intuitions are in that tradition. We're better off for it.

A Morality Abstract Enough for Everyone

I don't think many modern readers would enjoy living within the ancient Greek moral order. Ethics and social systems change radically over time, though there is a more timeless good by which they can be evaluated.

The Scottish philosopher Alasdair MacIntyre noted that even the term "good" can refer to things normally recognized as bad. It doesn't mean that these orientations are arbitrary but that the good is usually defined by a given social context, and social context changes. A society might strive toward something desirable within that society but not for humanity in general. Some modern philosophers have contrasted reason with emotion or desire in such a way that the ends were merely the outcome of nonrational passions, and reason could calculate only as the means to attain such ends.

We might broadly speak of the ages prior to Socrates as pre-Socratic. People in those times made no significant attempt to transcend time and place and describe a good for all humanity. So to speak, it was a world without reason, whereas Socrates and the Greek philosophers who came after him tried to tease out what humans should aim for, a good that would still appeal to the minds around you even if you traveled thousands of miles from home, though few people then did.

As history goes on, the tendency has been for morality to become more abstract, impartial, and universalized, but that process is not inevitable. There was once a world without reason, and if we're not careful and we let tribal or nationalistic bickering override appeals to our shared morality and rationality, we may return to it. The Greek city-states did fall, and so did their ethical language.

Rome was an entirely different animal. Greek city-states required close familial and personal bonds, but Rome was an empire that marched right over such close-knit communities. Rome required an altogether different moral and ethical vocabulary, and the good would be redefined again and again in Western history to fit the changing social and moral order.

Could we really return to such a crude pre-Socratic ethics today? In fact, we have. Many of my colleagues are fans of Karl Marx, but they cannot tell you a thing about his ethics. Ironically, Marx's class analysis followed the lead of Agamemnon, king in an age of warriors, not of commerce. For Marx, capitalists are bad and workers are good, not because of what they do but because of their social class and function. Whether you are good or not depends only on your social class. The proposed communist revolution was based on that ethical division. The terrible real-life results—for factory output, ordinary people's retirement planning, and mundane effects such as lowering prices—weren't central to his thinking.

Socrates did not think like a warrior. He didn't have a clearly defined "enemy," thank goodness. He also didn't have as complete a system as Plato would later construct, which may have made him less prone to envisioning radical political upheaval. Socrates had been able to articulate the foundational arguments necessary to define the good life, but Plato would spend his days pursuing arguments that could stand the test of time. Plato's first crucial insight was that we use the concept of good to evaluate possible objects of desire and aspiration. Hence the good cannot simply mean "whatever men desire"; there must be something beyond that.

As noted in the previous chapter, Plato believed that ideas are the most real aspects of life and objects in the physical world are merely passing, insubstantial entities. Ideas such as justice or the mathematical properties of geometry are everlasting and true, whereas rocks and trees fade over time. Plato would end up arguing that the philosopher could ascend to this realm of ideas or forms. One could reach pure ideas by dialectical thought, by going back and forth in the mind through deduction, and finally achieve "knowledge" of the forms. A specific dress is red, but where is the idea of red? It is in the Forms and can be known only by reason. For Plato, the end of human life, the goal, is metaphysical contemplation of transcendent truth (philosophy). Or, as Saint Augustine would later put it, contemplation of God in the Christian tradition.

To Socrates and the philosophers who followed in his immediate footsteps, justice was not just justice for a given city. There is knowledge to be acquired about ethics. Indeed, virtue is a form of knowledge.

This is not to say that local customs are irrelevant. Plato acknowledged that context and background assumptions are necessary for coherent ethical thought, a certain social order. The details of that shared picture must become more sketchy and abstract, though, when one moves beyond a given Greek city-state into the comparative vastness of the later Roman Empire.

The Roman Empire was vast by the standards of the day, and it remains one of the largest empires that ever existed. Woe to those who got in the way of that beast. As MacIntyre shows, the question was no longer what forms of social life exist nearby or even which virtues apply to imperial social life in general. Rather, the new question was: What must "I," as a man stripped of all social ties, do to be happy while there are Roman legions marching by at random and other large social forces that are well beyond my control (much larger than the empowering world of the Athenian democratic assembly)?

One answer would be Stoicism—virtue as acceptance of circumstances in a big, indifferent universe. In time, out of Rome and this cold ethical system would emerge the contrary warmth of Christian hope and love. But before the word becomes flesh, the word becomes a universal rational principle in Stoicism. Whether it is questing reason, cold reason, or universal wisdom, there must be something bigger than cities and happenstance. Stoicism remained important closer to our own era because it influenced many of the Founders of the United States, as well as Adam Smith, the father of modern economics. Like the universality of Christian ethical claims, it was part of the push away from the tribal to the abstract/universal. That's the long-term trend in ethics and many other areas of human thought.

In *A Short History of Ethics*, MacIntyre argued:

Both Epicureanism [not exactly hedonism but an emphasis on materialism] and Stoicism are convenient and consoling doctrines for private citizens of the large impersonal kingdoms and empires of the Hellenistic and Roman worlds. . . . Religion is thus manipulative (Roman terrors and pageantry), [and] the members of the middle and upper classes become unable to share the religion which they use for political purposes. They need beliefs which are rational by their own standards.

The Romans, more consciously than their tribal forebears, espoused certain philosophies for the sake of maintaining social order, even if they weren't terribly sure if those philosophies were true. The upper classes were relatively content to accept the existing social order in stoic fashion, but what about everyone else? As MacIntyre wrote, "Exposed to poverty, disease, death, and often enough their owners, they still question how they are to live and what virtue and what happiness might be in their case. For some of these the mystery religions provided an answer. For even more, an answer was to be given with the coming of Christianity." In a loveless empire, Christianity brought hope to those who needed it most. Apathy was fine for the rich; the lowest members of the social order needed love.

This class tension is not one we can attribute only to the decadent Romans; it was inherent in Greek philosophy as well. The ideal of the leisured and perfected life of abstract contemplation is accessible only to an elite, and it presupposes a class structure that excludes ordinary men from both political power and the moral idea. Stoicism lacked love, and Christianity delivered this virtue in full force, since God is love. God is Father. God is Son. God is personal.

This is not just the view of a Christian like me. Anyone familiar with philosophy will know that the atheist nineteenth-century philosopher Friedrich Nietzsche's chief assault on Christianity was over this very virtue, its emphasis on personal love. He did not confront Stoicism on those grounds; he attacked the religion and philosophy of love, since he thought it weakens man and makes him a sheep rather than a god.

When you see the nastiness of some of the thinkers influenced by Nietzsche (though not all are bad), including some fascists and deconstructionists, you have to conclude that his opposition to Christianity's boundless love was a dangerous mistake. Yet even today, there are plenty of thinkers who would be happy to complete Nietzsche's work, throwing out Christianity and the hard-won ethical developments that go with it. We have been discarding the Judeo-Christian tradition without providing a ready replacement.

That is not to say that our own era has become utterly cold-hearted. Quite the contrary. We still long for the sense of universal love, but detached from ethics and tradition it can become vapid and shallow. Think of the mushy compassion of the latest liberal advice guru you've seen on Oprah-style talk shows. There are worse things, including some brutal pre-Socratic warrior creeds, but our contemporary ethos is a bit unmoored. It has forgotten its own origins, so it takes love and peace for granted instead of seeing them as the tradition does. Want to see love? Look at God. Look at the Cross. That is one definition of love.

A love of the Western tradition enables us to see past its superficial contradictions and defend the whole instead of becoming fixated on one narrow aspect, such as hedonism alone or mere stoic duty. For most of our history after Plato, the Judeo-Christian tradition was the glue that helped keep society together.

Our Political History Is Filled with Theological Arguments

Our long Judeo-Christian tradition is not just dogma but the product of a centuries-long dialogue about what works—what creates happy, flourishing societies and individuals—and what doesn't. Taken as a whole, that tradition offers us what you might call *reason to have faith*. In Chapter 10 we'll examine the moral struggles of the early church thinker Saint Augustine, but first let's look ahead at some of the political implications of Christianity as they have worked themselves out in Western history.

Much of the ostensibly secular philosophy written since the early days of Christianity has really been a gradual playing out of premises implicit in Judaism and Christianity, particularly the worth of the individual and the need for a sphere of freedom of conscience. What was the eighteenth-century German philosopher Immanuel Kant's emphasis on the importance of treating each individual as an end unto himself if not a rationalist's version of the Golden Rule? Or utilitarianism if not the recognition that each individual's happiness matters regardless of rank or ancestry? Or libertarianism if not a secularized version of the West's tradition of freedom of conscience?

Moses was not buddies with Pharaoh, Jesus was not on good terms with Pontius Pilate. The position of being the religious rebel against governmental authority is the very backbone of Western tradition. God is the goal. God informs us about the good, and government is judged in that light by individuals who make decisions freely. We're independent thinkers because we are religious, not autocrats due to religion.

Just over six hundred years ago, the West went from freedom of conscience (as it was increasingly called) to political freedom, with a crucial further transition around 1400 to rights—mandatory claims that do not exist merely at the whim of a king or a noble. There was no word in any language for "rights" before 1400, not as we think of them, according to MacIntyre.[1] But there had been a long and increasingly influential tradition of tolerance, thank goodness.

Relentlessly intellectually honest, Augustine admitted he found justifications in scripture for *both* tolerance and force, and centuries later Saint Thomas Aquinas argued for limiting tolerance in many ways, especially in the face of heresy. But the historical pull toward tolerating the dissenter, the thoughtful loner, was already there, growing ever more formalized and better protected. Repressive as the twelfth century might look by our freewheeling standards, it saw a growing discussion of how best to tolerate multiple faiths— Christian, Jewish, and Muslim. Peter Abelard and Raimundus Lullus wrote interreligious dialogues searching for ways of defending the truth of Christian faith while also seeing some truth—religious or at least ethical—in other religions. In Judaism and Islam, this was mirrored by writers such as Moses Maimonides or Ibn-Rushd (also known as Averroës), whose defense of philosophical truth searching against religious dogma is arguably the most innovative of the period. Today we must be very careful to distinguish between Muslim individuals generally and those groups or governments who seek to do us harm.

Nicolas of Cusa's *De Pace Fidei* (1453) encouraged the ecumenical notion of one underlying religion approached via various rites. Cusa marks an important step toward a more comprehensive, Christian-humanist conception of toleration, though in the conversations among representatives of different faiths his core idea of "one religion in various rites" remains a Catholic one. Still, the search for common elements is a central, increasingly important topic in toleration discourses.

This is much further developed in Erasmus of Rotterdam's humanist idea of a possible religious unity based on a reduced core faith, which attempted to avoid religious strife about what Erasmus saw as nonessential questions of faith.[2] The historian George Marsden shows the possible logical implication of this intended "core" unity, though: we end up with no ethics at all. However, even this degree of tolerance was a welcomed improvement over the previous centuries of religious warfare. After Martin Luther and the Reformation—and even more the Treaty of Westphalia, which ended wars between Europe's empires in 1648—national states dominated Europe, and only in the twentieth century did they finally dominate the entire globe. Religious warfare as a driver of Western history was effectively at an end. States would commit all manner of violence, but alongside them rose the modern tradition of human rights. Luther helped by distinguishing between the spiritual realm and an earthly one where states ruled through coercion and thus had to be somehow morally bound.

The Twelve Articles of 1525, demands German peasants made to their rulers, is considered the first list of human rights in Europe. The year 1683 saw the British Bill of Rights. Today, dispensing with such guarantees—rooted in the value of the individual—is almost unthinkable. Yet so much of what we take for granted in the realm of political morality developed in the past few centuries from the deeper, older roots I have been discussing. The real recurring danger in Western history is not so much that religion will destroy rights but that absent the (largely religion-grounded or religion-spawned) rights tradition, we will drift back to the cynicism and brute force of Rome.

Religion is not the real threat. Even the stodgy Puritans who moved from Europe to North America believed in the separation of church and state. Building on their example, Roger Williams, the Puritan founder of Rhode Island, successfully argued that the state had no authority in religion's basic elements. James Madison, got his start at seminary. Again and again, it appears that the real conflict in the West is not between faith and rationality but between the helpful rules shaped by *both* religion and secular philosophy and the irrationality of untrammeled power, checked by *neither* faith nor reason.

(Contrary to what some socialists and religious believers might tell you, religious movements themselves tend to arise not from poverty but from the comfort and material well-being that affords quiet reflection. Thomas Aquinas and many other major religious thinkers came from wealthy families.)

I adhere to the views of the sixteenth-century French theologian John Calvin, who is in a sense one of the most unoriginal thinkers in the tradition but also one of the best because he sought to find and use the word of God, not his own word, in all his writings. He was trained as a humanist, and his systematic theology still stands as the foundation for most Protestant thought. His impact upon the Protestant tradition in the United States cannot be overstated. Harvard, Princeton, and Yale would grapple with the system he constructed. And yes, I think those views are perfectly in keeping with a love of freedom as we normally think of it. It was specifically Calvinist Puritan theology that led to the freest society on Earth when Roger Williams created the colony of Rhode Island on the explicit and then novel basis of toleration. The society required an absolute respect for individual conscience and liberty in the royal charter (as the shared moral criterion) promulgated in 1640. Williams predated Thomas Jefferson and the Deist camp by 150 years in what would become the United States, and he was the first to write on and implement the famous "Wall of Separation."

Williams also made revolutionary moves on slavery, private property, and the role of the church in society. His faith and reason directly informed the founding principles that have led to this nation's success. It doesn't mean that his faith is true, that you must believe it, or that I would compel you to believe it. In fact, that is the main message of his work and this book: you should be free to choose your faith and ethics. That is your right! It is God's moral foundation. God made you free, and you should make your own moral choices. Otherwise they are not moral.

Correspondingly, I would appreciate the space to make my own moral decisions without pressure from those who think they know better. That is the original liberal contract that gave us hope, but now it's cracking. The original liberals believed in liberty, free learning, and free living, and they wrote a Constitution based on those principles. Many liberals are no longer liberal. They coerce. They cannot name their ethics. The major question remaining is whether we can continue the American experiment without this moral foundation.

In conclusion, how significant is Roger Williams? David Little claims, "John Locke's ideas are simply restatements of the central arguments in favor of freedom of conscience developed by Roger Williams." Wilbur Kitchener Jordan, in his classic study *The Development of Religious Toleration in England*, concluded that not Locke's but Williams's "carefully reasoned argument for the complete dissociation of church and state . . . may be regarded as the most important contribution made during the century." Williams and Locke differed only in that Williams granted liberty to Catholics, which Locke did not, and Williams did not exclude atheists from liberty, which Locke explicitly did. In both instances, Locke denied certain groups freedom because he feared they would undermine the civil state. Not Williams.

Politics without Our Tradition Is Cultural Amnesia

So reason and religion were accepted as compatible moral foundations—really, elements of one foundation—by George Washington, James Madison, Adam Smith, Abraham Lincoln, and Martin Luther King, Jr., to name just a few. However, by 1900 major changes were taking place in academia, as noted earlier, and those changes would be felt in the broader culture by the 1960s. The Greatest Generation, which preceded the late 1940s to 1960s baby boomers, is still present at some of my public talks, and they cannot believe the transformation our ethics has taken. They are sad that ethics is fading, and I'm sorry to say that my lecture makes them even sadder. Martin Luther King, Jr., had a dream with specific spiritual content. Can anyone now name that content? He had a PhD in theology and ethical criteria that followed the grand tradition we are surveying. But few follow his criteria today.

For a civilization as vast as the one left behind in the collapse of the Roman Empire, there must be some shared ethos, and so it has been in functioning societies closer to our own day.

Madison was the great conciliator of the First Congress. He would need all his political capital to win the battle for the Bill of Rights. Madison took to the floor to introduce his draft on June 8, 1789. To quote Chris DeRose's *Founding Rivals: Madison vs. Monroe, the Bill of Rights, and the Election That Saved a Nation*, "His amendments are familiar to us all, and so fundamental to our national identity that we cannot imagine America without them: the freedom of speech and of the press . . . and on." No less an opponent than Patrick Henry would soon come around, as he wrote to Madison tendering the equivalent of his resignation as opponent-in-chief.

How could Madison's word be believed by the antifederalists? How could Madison be trusted on this ultimate issue of rights? Because it was Madison who had earlier sponsored the Virginia Statute of Religious Freedom and been the prime opponent of the dreaded "general assessment" that would have taxed all Virginians to support the Episcopal Church. In the end, Madison's sympathy for the Baptists and dissenters would be remembered and make all the difference. As DeRose put it, "His career-long advocacy of religious freedom had served as a powerful deposit on that promise, which might otherwise have been dismissed as an election-year conversion of convenience."[3]

So evident were James Madison's achievements, his monument at Montpelier reads simply MADISON, together with the dates of his birth and death. But he was not a man who invented an ethos out of whole cloth. Like all Western greats for centuries, he was a vessel of the Judeo-Christian ethos.

Ferguson's Six "Killer Apps" for Cultural Success

So if our roots were religious and modernity, which is overall a good thing, is secular and rights-oriented, what shared elements of reason and faith are the real keys to our success?

The historian Niall Ferguson picks six essential "apps"[4] that make Western civilization work: competition, science, property rights, medicine, the consumer society, and a work ethic. To reinforce those values, we have to talk about them in moralized terms. They cannot be an afterthought or taken for granted. Consider the rise in income in the past two centuries and ask yourself whether Western capitalism should be condemned as something immoral.

Niall Ferguson's Six "Killer Apps" of Western Civilization's Success

- Competition
- Science
- Property rights
- Medicine
- The consumer society
- A work ethic

I agree with the economic historian Deirdre McCloskey that capitalist modernity is in large part a product of a change in the moral rhetoric about commerce. It's troubling, then, that once again commerce has almost become a dirty word in modern American political discourse.

But even the archvillain in our story, the ultimate collectivist Karl Marx, was essentially a materialist prophet seeking to turn the egalitarian concern for the needy found in the Judeo-Christian tradition into a millenarian political urgency. His far subtler contemporary Alexis de Tocqueville better understood that the newfound freedom of nineteenth-century America offered humanity an unprecedented opportunity to reconcile individualism and participation in communities.

Just as free markets would make the United States the richest nation in history without central planning, so does the freedom to enter and exit society's many "little platoons"—its clubs, associations, movements, causes, and, yes, churches—allow a culture to flourish without a centrally dictated agenda. To Alasdair MacIntyre, "The paradox of Christian ethics is precisely that it has always tried to devise a code for society as a whole from pronouncements that were addressed to individuals or small communities meant to separate themselves from the rest of society."[5] So Christianity is well suited to a diverse society with its basic ground rules instead of thousands of detailed mandates.

But the skeptic understandably asks, "Why should I do what God commands?" To this, the Judeo-Christian tradition offers three kinds of answers. The first points to God's holiness, the second to his goodness, the third to his power. The presupposition of all three answers, though, is that worship is a rational activity. God in effect says to his followers, "Do not merely be silent and obey but let me persuade you."

Since all humans must be persuaded as individual, thinking minds, the notion of the equality of men before God has a moral content. It implies a type of community in which nobody has superior rights of a moral or a political kind, and need, not rank, is the criterion of one's claim upon other people. The community provides a framework for participants to realize the ideals for themselves and others; it is commended or condemned according to the quality of that framework, and the type of community is to be commended or condemned insofar as it provides a better or worse framework within which participants' ideals for themselves and for others can be realized.

Despite all the bad things done in its name at times, Christianity is at heart so tolerant—so intent on propagating moral beliefs and rules that facilitate ordinary human life for humble, ordinary human beings—that it has been content to accept conceptual frameworks from elsewhere, including Platonism. As religions go, Christianity isn't that pushy. It hopes you'll see the light if you are free to think it over for a while.

Saint Augustine, the fourth-century AD saint and theologian mentioned earlier, borrowed from the Platonic dichotomy between the world of sense perception and the realm of Forms, then Christianized the concept, envisioning a dichotomy between natural desires and divine order. Christianity as we know it is not old and barbaric but in some ways a refinement of the still respected foundational Western philosophy.

Eight centuries after Augustine, the Aristotelianism of Thomas Aquinas is interesting as well and tantalizingly more familiar, since it is concerned not merely with escaping from the snares of the world and desire but with transforming desire for moral ends. Nowadays we might almost say that Thomas was interested in "harnessing human desires for good ends." Thomas's theological ethics aimed to preserve the *non*-theological meaning of the word *good*: "Good is that to which desire tends."

Three centuries later, in the sixteenth century, the structure of Luther's ethics is best understood as follows: the only true moral rules are the divine commandments, and the divine commandments have no further rationale or justification than that they are the injunctions of God. This makes God out to be a bit impetuous. Thomas, you might say, had almost civilized Yahweh by offering rationales for God's rules that in theory everyone might agree upon. Luther turned God into the willful creature whom the eighteenth-century English poet William Blake would mock as an all-too-human-seeing character he dubbed "Nobodaddy." This could be considered the start of a modern trend toward being annoyed by the rules God imposes. Their underlying rationality is no longer emphasized.

Alasdair MacIntyre basically concludes, with a hint of the modern annoyance, that the only "criterion" for Christian ethics is that "God says so." God commands, and that is that. MacIntyre was a bit cranky at that period in his philosophy career, and some minor Marxist threads were likely creeping into his thinking. But his treatment of religion is very important to understand because it frames the way a lot of academics view religion as well.

For example, MacIntyre likes Thomas not because of his treatment of the Christian God, but rather because he shares the philosophical method of Aristotle, including Aristotle's emphasis on the idea that good means good for *humans*. As MacIntyre sees it, no God claims or revelations are thus necessary to create ethics in this modern world. God is now defined in terms of human concepts. His ethics are bound by what we desire, for good or for bad.

I don't think the God who thundered from Mount Sinai would quite share that view. The First Commandment pretty much makes that point: "Thou shalt have no other gods before me." MacIntyre knows this and wrote, "If one develops in detail the morality of St. Augustine . . . one is expounding theology, which appeals to revelation rather than a philosophical ethics." He then apologized for spending only ten pages on the history of Christianity, the most significant ethical system in human history. (He ignored Judaism altogether, a terrible omission.) Nevertheless, he is useful to read even about Christianity because what he says is rooted in history and fact, not tied to faith commitments, and he still ends up vindicating much of traditional Judeo-Christian thinking.

He understands my argument that history proves our old moral precepts work and are not arbitrary.

Taking the Judeo-Christian Tradition into the Wider World

Even at his most radical, Alasdair MacIntyre reveals the threads that connect Christianity to contemporary politics and economics.

It is interesting to see where he turns for solace when modern society disappoints him, as it does all of us from time to time. MacIntyre wishes we still lived in small Greek city-states with intimate social relations. He dislikes the modern individualized world of large nation-states and the market system that binds it together. His frustration is exactly what makes his line of thought so clear. He is not really mad at God; he is mad at Man. He shows what we have chosen, perhaps unwisely, and he illustrates our desires, our ends, and our ethics. He is not happy about our choices. Could it be that his own preferred system of ethics has partially caused such desires and choices?

If the sovereign God of the Judeo-Christian tradition is out, what is in? MacIntyre would say human reason, as do so many moderns, but that only raises another question: why can't we ever seem to follow reason? God has an answer to that, but reason does not.

On Christianity, MacIntyre explains that it is difficult to decipher exactly what Christian ethics looks like. I grant that this is true as a factual matter. Christianity is all over the map, especially at present. There are pro-life and pro-choice texts, both with plausible-sounding arguments. There are pro-gun and pro-gun-control Christians. There are pro-liberty and pro-big-government formulations. It is hard to claim that a clear Christian ethics emerges in practice today.

Jesus himself did not seem overly concerned with having a monopoly on such ethical claims. The Gospel was the forgiveness of sins, and the love of God consumed his teaching. In fact, he seemed to scorn certain types of legalists. But he did retain the law pretty firmly. Change the least bit of the Jewish Law, and you are better off at the bottom of the sea with a millstone around your neck. But Jesus certainly offered a new spin on the law: love is the Great Command; God's love, not sentimental human feelings.

In spite of these difficulties, we can still tease out some dominant ethical themes in Christianity, even ones with political relevance, and MacIntyre is quite objective in describing them. He sees no reason to quarrel with the contention that Christianity "introduced" (even more strongly than the Stoics did) the concept of every man as somehow equal before God. Even if this conviction appeared compatible with the institutions of slavery and serfdom, it also provided grounds for attacking those institutions whenever their abolition appeared remotely possible. No more assuming that because you are physically able to abuse other humans, you morally may.

The notion of the equality of men before God has moral content, implying a type of human community in which nobody has superior moral or political rights to anyone else. "In fact," wrote MacIntyre, "the distinctive values of equality and of the criteria of need which Christianity in large part begot could not possibly commend themselves as general values for human life until it began to appear possible for the basic material inequalities of human life to be abolished." That is to say, moral rules can't apply until there is at least some hope of real human beings adhering to those rules. MacIntyre thinks that "it is only in small, separated communities that values of fraternity and equality can be incarnated; they cannot provide a program for society as a whole."

In other words, he understands that the Judeo-Christian tradition raised the moral bar, set a new standard for humanity, but he doesn't really believe that that admirable standard is compatible with the individualistic, capitalistic modern world; we must retreat to something more like village life. That would be bad news, but I hope to show that markets and morals are still mutually supportive if we can get through the current crisis in ethics and politics.

Sharing Family Traditions, Like Them or Not

MacIntyre argues that both Jesus and St. Paul preached an ethics devised for a short interim period before God finally inaugurated the Messianic Kingdom. "It is therefore not surprising that insofar as Christianity has propounded moral beliefs . . . it has been content to accept conceptual frameworks from elsewhere, including

Feudal concepts of hierarchy and role, Platonic Forms as Christianized by St. Augustine with humanity now receiving illumination not from the Forms but from God, and finally . . . Aquinas who brought the Vision of God as the goal of human desire, the list of virtues, and a framework of law which has both Stoic and Hebraic origins."

When MacIntyre is not busy mocking Calvinists for their purported willingness to accept even nonrational edicts from God, he provides helpful truths to make sense of the complex set of ethical concepts offered above. No sentence is perhaps as important as this one: "The presupposition of the use of such concepts [by Christians] is that worship is a rational activity." The New Testament is framed as important information, the good word, and God is defined as an adequate object of worship. The West is the story of the continuous unfolding of this rational Judeo-Christian set of assumptions, though working out the details takes centuries, possibly an eternity. No perfect story of ethics has ever been written. We struggle within this tradition as do those in other traditions.

But we struggle with human reason at the center of our debates, though not blindly. We are fallen, but we have the Word as a sort of life raft if we can figure out how to operate it together. The Jews and their rabbis basically originated and defined good theological and philosophical debate in their ancient struggles with these issues. (It is tempting to see the proportion of Nobel Prizes in science and other honors going to Jewish intellectuals as empirical proof that they are chosen for a special place in our history. But as I tell my students, if you examine those who are chosen by God, I'm not sure how many of you would want the honor. It is a tough calling. Read the Bible.)

So MacIntyre starts out sounding cynical, with an absolutist God uttering almost petty commands, but then he sees the immense role for reason in Christian ethics, and of course this is correct. Recall that theologians founded Harvard, Oxford, Cambridge, and the aforementioned Princeton. The Judeo-Christian tradition is neither complete nor perfect, but it did the heavy lifting in the West when it comes to promulgating core principles such as the equality of all people (because we are all created in the image of God) and the criterion of need for determining where our social/moral attention must be directed. If we are all children of God, human need cries out to God's ears. That is the story. God hears those who are in bondage. Justice is at hand, for God is a loving God (but God is also a jealous God visiting his wrath upon those who hate him).

Other elements of the faithful life will improve the ethics of an individual or a nation. But the core concepts of equality and need are all that's necessary to understand the rise of modern political philosophies in recent centuries. It's shocking how powerful these two reasonable criteria can be in shaping the political intuitions of contemporary people. For all the criticisms some of us heap upon President Obama, he still unapologetically declares that inalienable rights come from God, our Creator. With that foundation still in place, there is much good work that can be done and a thriving, still widely shared Judeo-Christian moral/political tradition upon which to draw.

The real thesis of this book is that the economic history of the United States and even our current moral debates stick precisely to those centuries-old themes. However, current talking heads make justice claims invoking equality and need that have no foundation in God or Judeo-Christian ethics. It seems certain that another ethics could evolve with such core concepts, but to date this has not happened. What is the name of that replacement system, if modern activists have one to offer?

Communism ensured equality of sorts and promised to meet human need, but interestingly all you had to do was give up on God. Communism seems to be a jealous god. The central planners, once they began to rise, wanted to be fundamental in the story that is history. Trying to achieve that, they wiped out religion, freedom of conscience, and the free press. Without God as a foundation, far from making society more humane, there is a danger that rights and equality will fade into the normal narrative of human history with all its horrors and yield a war of all against all as its next chapter. How well would human need be met amid the barbaric conditions that have prevailed throughout most of history?

We currently have abundance beyond historical comprehension. This can end. We are promised many versions of hope and change, but there is only one version that has worked thus far. Without it, the poor likely will not prosper, and the rest of humanity will not be much better off, if any of us survive.

Big Arguments within a Shared Moral Vocabulary

The esteemed New Testament scholar Richard Hays might disagree with my story a bit. He says that "rights" do not exist in the New Testament narrative, and he is correct. I cannot argue. However, he also implies that rights claims may not be fundamental to the Christian community and tradition, and I am not ready to join him in that view. Hays lays out the utopian call of Jesus in the Sermon on the Mount, and he says it is not optional, no matter how spectacularly awry utopian planning has gone in the real world. No matter how impractical, he wrote, we must continue "articulating the concrete implications of the Word of God for the community of faith."[6] I agree in part, but I think he has missed one crucial dimension of the Christian story.

My grandmother used to say, "The Devil can cite Scripture to his purpose." Or, as we might put it in academia, "The biblical text has inexhaustible hermeneutical potential." For Hays, the 1988 presidential election offered a vivid illustration as two Christian ministers ran for the presidency: Jesse Jackson and Pat Robertson, each declaring the Bible as the grounds of his convictions, championing widely divergent visions of Christian morality. Everybody wants to claim the Bible, but to make that happen Hays thinks we must put aside all contemporary politics, reject modern society, as it were, and appeal instead only to the self-consciously Christian community, telling the story of the Cross and witnessing the world as a New Creation since the coming of Christ.

I'm a little more optimistic about our ability to engage in some course correction. Jackson and Robertson weren't complete outsiders to current American politics. For all their disagreements, they were reminders that we still conduct our arguments within a broader shared context of Judeo-Christian or at least heavily Judeo-Christian moral norms and assumptions. We rarely dare to label it as such in an overt way because we are rightly cautious of alienating people who are not conscious participants in that great tradition. Nonetheless, it remains our shared social context, as Aristotle, Taylor, and MacIntyre might all agree.

We share a tradition, and within that tradition we have room to argue. That's how the Judeo-Christian tradition has worked for millennia. The one-rigid-plan-for-all method of a Rousseau or for that matter Stalin is not our way. I hope it never will be, though the danger is always there.

The truth is, politics has really become the remaining battlefield of ideas in Judeo-Christian-influenced Western civilization. Broad theological agreement has basically been achieved. At times the pope even reaches out to Islam and other faiths to emphasize the underlying desire of all faiths to seek guidance from God. The political implications of faith, even within Christianity, remain hotly contested. But even those political divisions become easier to navigate if we admit that they're taking place within a Judeo-Christian context. More unites us than divides us, as they say.

I understand the frustration of would-be rationalists who want to ditch tradition because they think it gets in the way. Luckily, there are rational social theorists who understand how religion can be helpful, including the economist Friedrich Hayek, who was not religious himself but recognized how rationalists owed a debt to people of faith for maintaining norms such as adherence to property rights that enable society to function without waiting for economists to come along and explain it all.

One of the most important intellectuals to eliminate the sentiments and traditions that preceded him and attempt to judge political decisions by their immediate, observable benefits was Niccolò Machiavelli in the early 1500s. Like the sophists before him and somewhat like the Romans at their most cynical, he defended the weaving of public lies and deployment of what we would now call propaganda as long as it helped shore up the monarch and kept the republic stable. His intentions were not evil, but there is a reason his last name has given us an adjective that implies unprincipled manipulation.

Once the West began making rational calculations of public benefit without regard to long-standing moral principle, without the backbone of tradition, the way was opened for innovations both useful and dangerous. The Enlightenment grab bag of economic and scientific analysis could lead either to lasting freedom or to revolutionary Marxist fantasies and, even in freer societies, lots of burdensome economic regulations gussied up in the language of utilitarianism even as they spread misery.

In a sense, modernity and its cynicism started around the time of Machiavelli, only a century or so after the individual rights language now essential to our freedom was born. We have inherited it all. The most dangerous part of that bundled inheritance is when the rationalists create everything from scratch without regard to tradition—like all-seeing gods operating without intermediary institutions—and eliminate anything standing in the way of their vaunted plans, leaving humans with few community ties and sentimental attachments. The Absolute Individual confronts the Absolute State on a stark plane of pure theory.

This is no idle fear. The topic of our next chapter and the immense problem confronting us in Washington, DC, today is the rise of the modern super-state, with all its dangers. The present offers no escape from history.

chapter eight

TRIBE, NATION, EMPIRE, AND IMMIGRATION

I love all God's children; ambitious or grandiose as it sounds, I want what's best for all people around the world. That does not mean abandoning either our traditions or our unique national cultures, though. Reasonable restrictions on immigration may be best for everyone.

The United Nations is fond of the phrase "transcend national boundaries." The large, boring, expensive bureaucracy does not inspire much love. By contrast, the United States is still loved by most of its inhabitants. We protect the things we love. We care about their boundaries. I came to Washington promising, among my foremost duties, to take border security seriously. If we consider the United States a nation worth protecting, that duty is second nature. When we stop thinking of our country as something that inspires love—when it is just admission quotas and arbitrary boundaries, part of the profit-and-loss statements of transnational corporations—we risk becoming indifferent to its place in the larger international order.

Our moral commitments are tied to our sense of belonging and to a certain degree our sense of place, something the ancient Romans slowly forgot, to their regret. You often hear modern nations going through crises being compared to Rome in its final stages. It makes a disturbing amount of sense.

Rome was ravaged by a fire in 64 AD. The emperor Nero was rumored to have started it himself or to have sung "The Sack of Ilium" during the blaze (an incident later transformed in popular legend into him playing a lyre or fiddle, though the fiddle wouldn't be invented for about another thousand years).

Nero may not have wanted Rome to burn, but he seized the opportunity to rebuild the city more to his liking. He poured money into massive public works projects, including a palace, vineyards, an artificial lake, a giant statue of himself—all partly intended to create jobs to aid the poor. Like today's Federal Reserve, churning out ever more dollars but in the process lowering the value of each individual dollar, Nero paid for his government projects in part by debasing the Roman currency, making it much easier for the Roman government to (nominally) pay its bills but with less valuable coins. Nero wasn't too ashamed of those cheapened coins, though; he had them emblazoned with pictures of himself giving alms to the poor.

That program of government spending and money debasing worked out about as well for the Romans as it likely will for us: it created a short-term boom and delusional euphoria followed by a big, big economic decline—the start, really, of Rome's centuries-long slide from greatness to disintegration. It's unfortunate that the phrase "Roman Empire" looms so large in the modern mind because Rome's greatness, like our own, in many ways lies in the centuries during which it was a *republic*.

Overspending and debasing the currency were not the only parallels to our own day. The growing aggrandizement of the emperors coincided with a spiritual weakening in Rome. Recall in the previous chapter that I said there was a cynical awareness in Rome that religion was used for civic purposes rather than a full moral engagement with the reality of the cosmos, a true relationship between humans and the divine. No amount of "bread and circuses," as the Roman poet Juvenal would later put it, could disguise Rome's economic or spiritual weakness.

Then as now, nongovernmental institutions—civil society—filled the void, and many of them were Christian, easing the transition that occurred under Emperor Constantine in the early fourth century AD toward making Rome a Christian empire. (It was officially declared a Christian empire by one of his successors in 380 AD.) I am no fan of making the tax code byzantine (so to speak), but there was a certain wisdom in the emphasis President George W. Bush placed on "faith-based institutions" as a more efficient substitute for certain welfare services.

It is as if people sense that the kind of heartlessness that existed both in Rome and our own overbureaucratized aid institutions goes hand in hand with the inefficacy of those institutions. A heartless bureaucracy can reallocate money, but it cannot change the human heart or make wise judgments about which community members are in the most pain or display the greatest need. When large, impersonal bureaucracies fail, it is natural for people to turn to the little platoons of church congregations as a means of renewal. Instead of embodying the peak of a civilization, vast monuments may signal its approaching end. Grandiose architectural successes may be a sign of spiritual and cultural failure.

History Shows That Immigration Can Change Everything

One of Western history's great ironies is that the Germans, who would eventually see themselves as the heart of Continental civilization, began as comparatively uncivilized hordes pressing westward at the boundaries of the Roman Empire. They were literal barbarians for some four centuries after Christianity was declared Rome's official religion. Originally waves of distinct tribes of Vandals, Saxons, Goths, and other peoples, the Germans would eventually, of course, cohere into a nation-state.

Throughout the centuries, while Roman rule was being displaced by Germanic tribal law, Europe remained predominantly Christian and Christianized the incoming tribes, the transformation of souls and morals becoming more important than the mere physical migration. As Rome disintegrated, "Christendom" endured. Still, those invading hordes remain a stark reminder that even grand empires can collapse if they have no control over their borders and allow themselves to be looted.

In a further historical irony, Germany, reunified less than three decades ago in 1990 after its Cold War division, is now at the center of debate over how to handle large-scale migration, as hundreds of thousands of refugees from the Middle East and northern Africa arrive. Immigration and the right of a sovereign state to control it at the border was a central theme of my election campaign, in addition to the problem, even within the Republican Party, of leadership ignoring voters' concerns about immigration.

Voters—not to mention presidential candidates—concerned about immigration are sometimes condemned as xenophobes. Yet the very real gang violence, sexual assaults, and looting that accompanied the massive Muslim influx into Europe circa 2015—

including the horrific attacks in Cologne and elsewhere at the end of that year—are reminders that not every arriving band of immigrants has the same good intentions.

Furthermore, the current wave of new arrivals in Europe may be far less likely to convert to Christianity than the Goths of old. That doesn't mean Christianity ought to be a precondition for European or US citizenship, but some of the moral and legal norms Christianity helped spread may not be as universal as we might wish. The current migrants are not Islam's first incursion into the West, either, as the Spanish conquest by the Moors and the waxing and waning eastern borders during the Crusades remind us. The mass relocation of peoples and cultures can have immense consequences, reshaping history itself.

It is unfair to the most vulnerable members of Western societies for our elites to tell them that immigration is a painless process of seamless integration. By full open-border standards, of course there are some controls on immigration and the granting of refugee status, here as in Europe. But immigration bureaucracies and border guards are easily overwhelmed by large enough numbers, when guards even exist. The full implications of immigration still go mostly unexamined here, as in Europe, even in the midst of migrant crises and heated political debates.

Wherever you stand on immigration, three implications of mass immigration you ought to keep in mind are:

- *The immediate security effects.* Most immigrants are indeed coming here seeking work or reunion with extended family members, but right now we also face real, ongoing violent threats from both Islamic radicals and Latin American drug cartels.

- *The short-term economic effects.* As an economist, I know
  that immigration, like free trade, can yield long-term
  benefits (from the more efficient location of workers to the
  arrival of naturalized-citizen inventors and entrepreneurs).
  But those potential benefits do not magically eliminate the
  short-term dislocations for low-paid American workers and
  the unemployed if they suddenly find themselves competing
  with—and in effect underbid by—a huge new supply of
  unskilled, low-paid workers from abroad, mainly Latin
  America. Also, some open-border advocates say the GDP
  will increase as we add workers. Of course it will. But no one
  cares about GDP in total. We all care about GDP per person
  after taxes. Pretty simple.
- *The long-term cultural effects.* The immigrants of centuries
  past arrived in the United States knowing they would have
  to work to support their families and, consciously or not,
  adopt all the virtues of thrift and personal responsibility that
  go with it. Most of them also brought with them or adopted
  European-derived notions of respect for individual rights
  and, increasingly in recent decades, for women as equals
  under the law. What will become of the already debt-saddled
  and overburdened Western welfare states if newer waves of
  immigrants arrive expecting state-subsidized handouts and
  vote in ways that might diminish our freedom?

As the economist Milton Friedman noted long ago, open borders might have worked without the large modern bureaucratic welfare state. But with it, no way. And the world has changed with ISIS
and the technological warfare on the Web.

The dominant issue in the presidential polls this year is the nexus between national security, terrorism (one thousand open FBI terror cases across fifty states), immigration, and the refugee crisis. The candidates who listen to the people are in the lead. Perhaps there is hope after all.

The United States is large, and it is understandable that some of its 330 million inhabitants are not alarmed about the current immigration influx. But would you really expect, say, Denmark's population of 5.7 million, smaller than the population of New York City, to be as blasé in the face of hundreds of thousands of antidemocratic, unvetted voters joining their society?

It is unfortunate that we still aren't having a full, intellectually honest conversation in the United States about the costs and benefits of immigration. The politically correct taboo against examining the topic contributes to the average voter's sense that he's being left high and dry by the policy elites in Washington, including the Republican elites. Too often, even members of my own party have talked tough about border security in public only to work quietly toward amnesty for all illegal immigrants behind closed doors in Congress, partly due to big corporations' hunger for cheap labor. The more potential workers, the lower the wages, at least in the short term. This year we passed a veto-proof refugee bill, and somehow it didn't end up in the budget. But a 400 percent increase in H2B visas (visas for temporary seasonal nonagricultural workers) did make it in without a vote.[1] Then the elites want to know why voters are angry.

Even the Spanish-language version of the Republican Party's official response to the 2016 State of the Union address contained slightly different wording than the English version. It implied the need for immigration reform that would help the undocumented stop living in "the shadows," presumably by making them legal. But the original English-language version, delivered by South Carolina governor Nikki Haley, emphasized border security. People may not agree on the statistics regarding wages and population growth, but they notice double-talk, and they tend to get suspicious. I don't blame them.

If even the Republican Party secretly scoffs at border security, an angry public begins to feel it has nowhere to turn.

The Judeo-Christian Ethos Is Bigger Than a Single Tribe

One of the major tasks of modern nation-states—countries roughly as we know them and as they began to coalesce in Europe in approximately the thousand years after the fall of Rome, from about 500 to 1500 AD—was to foster loyalty to some entity larger than a tribe or ethnic group but smaller than an empire. If nations are to survive, they require internal ties more abstract and legalistic than "blood" but more concrete and traditionalistic than, say, "global commerce."

Luckily, both reason—in the sense common to the modern, scientific era that is the past five centuries—and the Judeo-Christian ethos occupy that sort of middle ground. Judaism was tied to a single tribe, but it placed much emphasis on an abstract law applied to all people by a single God. Over the centuries it would adapt to the diaspora that sent Jews scattering around the globe, working to maintain tradition and law without being anchored to one place. Christianity appeals to each individual mind in a way that transcends borders and bloodlines. It is truly open to anyone, of any social rank, in any time or place. Reason calls us to examine results and arguments, sharing them within a community of discussants.

These strands of the Western tradition escape the narrow confines of one small tribe, Germanic or otherwise, holding all to a shared standard higher than any petty chieftain. At the same time, the strands appeal to each individual mind, making them appropriate for a society built on the loyalty of its citizenry, and thus the loveless vastness of callous Rome is avoided. One can be a citizen of a country without being the heir of a specific family or at constant risk of being lost without social ties or status in some distant port.

Constitutions and Universal Rules

Constitutionalism, the fruit of centuries of European bargaining between rulers and ruled, is also a healthy intermediary social organizing principle. It's more abstract than blood ties but more local in application than "international law," over which individual citizens of any given nation have little direct influence. Constitutional law is an abstraction we share, and its direct influence on everyday life is sometimes palpable, making a single citizenry of diverse individuals who recognize that the chance for everyone to prosper is rooted in ground rules.

Contrast that happy potential to the less lofty phenomenon of ethnic "balkanization," each tribe hewing to its own ways and rules without feeling for those beyond the tribe or showing a strong interest in shared, transethnic norms. If you value constitutionalism— every liberal, conservative, and libertarian alike should, since all are invested in the rule of law—you have to acknowledge that mass immigration brings the risk of balkanization and thus the undermining of loyalty to society's rules. For most of its history the United States has been fortunate in functioning as a so-called melting pot, and there is no need for all immigrant populations to adopt the same mode of dress or attend the same church. But there is a risk in displaced loyalty to the broader society and adherence to national laws when a concept such as the sharia law of tribal loyalty is so intense. Sharia law lays out an elaborate set of legal principles governing almost all relations between Muslims, from marriage to business, such that in theory their disputes will almost never be matters for the courts of the broader society.

One significant movement of modern history has been the transformation of loyalty to a tribe into loyalty to the central state, with a constitution as its almost sacred credo. This is a highly efficient solution to the problem of diverse, but not quite imperially distant and far-flung, populations. However, this solution has its own dangers, subtler than being driven westward by the Huns sixteen hundred years ago but still troublesome. For instance, the citizens of a nation-state do not have the same built-in loyalty to its traditions that a family inevitably does to its tribe. The nation-state's unifying traditions require more conscious maintenance.

That's where an awareness of Western history—and the Judeo-Christian tradition that is its backbone—can be so helpful. It's like the DNA of our shared citizenship. The danger with an ignorant or forgetful nation-state populace is that without living moral and even aesthetic traditions, it's unified only by state propaganda. The government is the one thing all citizens of the nation-state share and to which they are loyal, if they are loyal to anything at all. It's a formula for the state's self-aggrandizement, and we may have reached that point some time ago. The Pledge of Allegiance is a lovely thing, but it was written by a nineteenth-century socialist to foster loyalty to government, and I would hate to see that sort of thinking prevail over richer, more neighborly Judeo-Christian values. And obviously modern nation-states have at times offered credos and causes far darker than the pledge. For instance, what was

Nazism, if not primitive (and in fact Germanic) tribal loyalty projected onto the heartless apparatus of the nation-state?

We want to avoid blind loyalty to the state while inculcating a sense that it exists within a background, a social context, and a tradition giving it moral and experiential weight. The United States should not just be the parcel of land we happen to live on, interchangeable with any other and open to any passersby who want to tarry or mooch here awhile. It has a history, and it is a product of that history. And that history has taught us things that vindicate the United States' existence and its specific (nonarbitrary) laws and social practices.

While sometimes defining itself against the Old World, the United States is also an outgrowth of European history, of Christendom. We are heirs to the lessons of Greece and Rome in a way that we are not per se heirs to the lessons of Confucianism, though that is no slight to Confucianism. Learning from our own history— and seeing how current practices were honed as our bad ideas were brutally weeded out—ties our personal experience to an organic national ethos, which grows in part from Europe and in turn rests within the broader Judeo-Christian tradition. Forget all that, and we are little better than amnesiacs wandering in North America; we might as well be North Koreans.

For centuries, sects have struggled to take the things that are good in their own customs and make them universalizable to all society and all populations. The goal of Christianity had been to create good individuals ready to face eternity no matter where they began socially or geographically rather than remake their surroundings according to a narrow political blueprint. To the extent that Christianity did remake society, observed the economist Douglass North, it did more through establishing intermediary, often local institutions—Burke's "little platoons"[2]—than by seizing the political high ground of throne or legislature and issuing commands to the populace. This is a philosophy that can travel.

Being conscious of a broader Western civilization of which we are a subset is useful for connecting us to goings-on in the wider world without turning us into an empire. We do not want a restoration of the loveless and vast Roman Empire and probably ought to be skeptical even about the sustainability of the European Union. However, we should know enough about the world to see European traditions as akin to our own, often in good ways. Like us, Europe at its best has embodied those six "killer apps" that Niall Ferguson identified: competition, science, property rights, medicine, the consumer society, and a work ethic.

The sense of a recognizable West is never more valuable than when its values are threatened with annihilation, as during the wars waged against them by the twin threats of fascism and communism. Those were more than geographic, territorial battles. Far more important, they were battles over the survival of a Western moral tradition—at times played out in locations far removed from Europe and fought by people who were not European. When we forget our moral traditions, we risk forgetting why some of the most important battles in history were fought. Then they will have been fought for nothing and may even be lost long after the apparent cessation of hostilities.

Let's take a look at the most terrible of those battles—World War II—and at its implications for our ability to defend ourselves today as we face groups such as ISIS and anti-Western leaders such as those in Iran.

chapter nine

NOT JUST PLAYING
DEFENSE

The Constitution gives the federal government no greater role than the defense of the American people. I strongly support a vigorous national defense that provides our armed forces with the resources necessary to protect against threats to our national security and the homeland. Potential threats on the horizon now include, but are not limited to, China, Russia, ISIS, Iran, and North Korea. Each challenges us not just with guns or bombs but with a philosophy antithetical to the individualist, freedom-oriented ethos I have been describing.

The importance of defending freedom—not just for us but for all humanity—makes it all the more worrying that if we do not put our fiscal house in order, it will become increasingly difficult to afford a strong military. With mandatory programs such as Medicare already consuming about 70 percent of the federal budget, we have at most 30 percent to spend on defense, but it competes with every other minuscule item in the budget. Currently, just over half of that discretionary spending, or about 16 percent of the entire federal budget, is spent on defense.[1] Though we have the finest military in the world, many of our vehicles and weapon systems are not in the state of fighting readiness they should be, especially not if they face multiple simultaneous conflicts.

Meanwhile, China and Russia are modernizing their forces, a skittish North Korea is expending much of its national wealth on its military, and the Arab world as well as Iran is producing an array of terrorist sects. We should love peace, but we cannot deny the existence of those threats. It is not loving to let free men and women be slaughtered if we can prevent it.

According to the *Army Times*, in 2015 Army Chief of Staff General Ray Odierno said, "The unrelenting budget impasse has compelled us to degrade readiness to historically low levels." He warned, "Even today we only have 33 percent of our brigades ready, when our sustained rate should be closer to 70 percent. We are unable to generate readiness for unknown contingencies, and under our current budget Army readiness will at best flatline over the next three to four years."[2] You can be sure our enemies are noticing, just as bin Laden noticed that "bleeding" the West economically can undermine our military resolve.

Compare that state of affairs to the mid–twentieth century, when the United States was the proud arsenal of democracy, guaranteeing freedom around the globe. Once we had the wealth to attempt projects such as the Marshall Plan, the rebuilding and defense of Europe after World War II, with an implicit warning to the Soviet Union not to reshape the ravaged Western Europe. With our economy faltering and our budget priorities askew, how could we ever hope to replicate such a world-altering feat today? We helped remake the constitutions of Germany and Japan after the war, and now we barely abide by our own. But we never would have had the opportunity to restructure those nations for the better if we hadn't had the military wherewithal to defeat them first.

An assessment by the Heritage Foundation of our military branches' readiness to fight two simultaneous major regional conflicts found that most are barely capable of it, military expenditures are shrinking as a percentage of GDP, and defense spending levels are now far below not only the Defense Department's request but even below the spending requests of President Obama. (See the following charts from the Heritage Foundation report.)

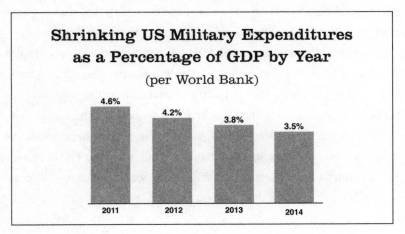

U.S. Military Power

	VERY WEAK	WEAK	MARGINAL	STRONG	VERY STRONG
ARMY		✔			
NAVY			✔		
AIR FORCE			✔		
MARINE CORPS			✔		
NUCLEAR			✔		
OVERALL			✔		

Shrinking US Military Expenditures as a Percentage of GDP by Year
(per World Bank)

4.6% 2011
4.2% 2012
3.8% 2013
3.5% 2014

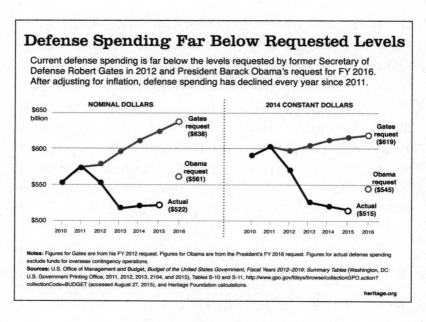

Defense Spending Far Below Requested Levels

Current defense spending is far below the levels requested by former Secretary of Defense Robert Gates in 2012 and President Barack Obama's request for FY 2016. After adjusting for inflation, defense spending has declined every year since 2011.

Notes: Figures for Gates are from his FY 2012 request. Figures for Obama are from the President's FY 2016 request. Figures for actual defense spending exclude funds for overseas contingency operations.

Sources: U.S. Office of Management and Budget, *Budget of the United States Government, Fiscal Years 2012–2016: Summary Tables* (Washington, DC: U.S. Government Printing Office, 2011, 2012, 2013, 2104, and 2015), Tables S-10 and S-11, http://www.gpo.gov/fdsys/browse/collectionGPO.action?collectionCode=BUDGET (accessed August 27, 2015), and Heritage Foundation calculations.

heritage.org

I am proud of and grateful for the men and women in uniform, including many near me in the Seventh District, who serve around the world to protect the freedom of the people of the United States. They and their families deserve our thanks for and admiration of their sacrifices. As a representative, I am committed to making sure they have everything they need to carry out their missions.

Keeping this nation safe, free, and prosperous is a complex undertaking. I will continue to actively advance Americans' security. I have sponsored efforts to improve border security, protect the homeland, and ensure that the armed forces have the capacity to act anywhere the United States' vital interests are threatened. We must defend ourselves against attacks while growing the economy to maintain a free, open society, in which we can secure the blessings of liberty for ourselves and our posterity.

I believe in a strong defense. When people remember that defense against foreign foes is a bedrock principle and the primary purpose of the modern nation-state, it causes them to be a bit less likely to vacillate in foreign policy decisions. That doesn't mean looking for a fight, blundering into every possible conflict, though.

Fewer than twenty-four hours after my 2014 primary victory, Chuck Todd wanted to pin me down as either an interventionist or an isolationist on military matters, hoping to pit me against other Republicans. Plenty of Republicans would have played right into his hands. I told him that for the moment I wanted to talk only about the election.

Both politicians and the media have a tendency to reduce complex issues to sound bites and slogans, but there are few issues that are more dangerous when robbed of all nuance than foreign policy. Economics is tough enough to teach, but at least that has a few basic laws. Foreign policy really has no such patterns, nothing as deductive as the laws of economics.

However, we can once more look to our history. The United States was founded on moral and philosophical principles including individualism and limited government. I'm afraid our shining example to the world was not enough to keep us safe. The French army had to add its might to the Colonial forces during our Revolutionary War to fend off the British. Only twenty-nine years after the Revolutionary War ended, the United States was again fighting for its survival against the British in the War of 1812, with the White House burned to the ground by the Brits in 1814.

There are sound reasons that the Founders were wary of war, but they also knew we would have to defend ourselves from time to time. So it is in a fallen world.

The Constitution says that Congress must reauthorize military spending every two years, which some people of a pacifistic bent have taken to mean that the United States should have no standing army at all. Given how frequently even the earliest presidents had to dispatch troops, it seems more likely that the Founders wanted to be sure the legislature retained the purse strings—and the power to declare wars—so that perpetual war would not be the prerogative of the president.

But when should the military be deployed? Once more, though religion has been falsely scapegoated as the main cause of history's wars (religion is just one of many things people fight over, from resources to language groups), the Judeo-Christian tradition provides firm guidance for the modern, mechanized society born of it. Catholic theologians were instrumental in devising "just-war" theory, and its conclusions are quite similar to the ones limited-government advocates draw about interpersonal and domestic-policy disputes. In essence: initiating violence is wrong, but preempting or retaliating against it is (often) appropriate.

That doesn't mean the United States should abandon its century-old role as a leader in world affairs or that it must intervene in every foreign conflict. The world is filled with trouble spots, and there's nothing conservative about wading into all of them, thinking we can single-handedly sort out complex local squabbles and depleting our own treasury while we're at it, and more important getting US troops killed. Also, we must never forget the many tools at our disposal for influencing world affairs in a profreedom way, not just the military. We have diplomacy, the amazing transformative power of trade, and our often imitated cultural example.

However, the government, if it has any legitimate function at all, is surely supposed to defend it citizens against violence. The government needs to destroy threats not only at the border, as discussed in the previous chapter, but within those borders—as in the case of terrorist attacks—and far beyond if the burgeoning threat is likely to harm Americans at home or overseas. History shows us that weakness invites attack, and it is not responsible to encourage our enemies to attack. (Note that the traditionally antiwar Catholic Church, which played a role in just-war theory, has given its blessing to rooting out al-Qaeda and ISIS terror cells. The Church is not pacifist, and neither is Western civilization.)

Once again, the best way to guide present-day policy is to remember that pragmatism and moral principle go hand in hand. When there is no compelling US interest in intervening in a local conflict and no side in the fight with a morally superior case, we would do well to stay out. The best candidates for US intervention are conflicts with a clearly defined, aggressing foe with an ideology opposed to the freedom philosophy our country espouses.

The United States tends to be at its worst when intervening with no clear-cut, principled purpose—as was arguably the case in its nineteenth-century wars with Mexico and Spain—and at its best when fighting battles to which morally attentive people around the world are tempted to rally if someone leads with courage.

Consider World War II.

Fighting on Land, at Sea, and in the Mind

The United States was in no rush to get involved in World War II, especially after the morass of World War I. (Prior to the sinking of the British ocean liner *Lusitania* and plenty of war propaganda from Woodrow Wilson and Madison Avenue, no small portion of Americans argued that we should have sided with the Germans against the English.) But Nazi ideology was a threat to more than

Germany's immediate neighbors. Imperial Japan was the immediate cause of our entry into the war, but Nazism was the real threat to European civilization, not just militarily but philosophically.

To individualism, the Nazis' response was the master race. To the study of history, the Nazis' response was conscious myth making, complete with knight imagery and tales of lost magical cities. To science, pseudoscientific racism. To limited government, the all-powerful state. To truth telling, the "big lie" of Goebbels's propaganda. To peace, war. To Christianity, elements of Norse paganism. To Judaism, death.

That's why World War II and the memory of its veterans continue to inspire us in a way that other conflicts do not—not to belittle any veterans who risked their lives for our nation. But even people without detailed political philosophies sense that there was a special darkness moving across the world in the Nazi threat. It's also one example of why a nuanced position on foreign policy still demands a strong military and recognition of the United States' place in the broader context of the West. We must be powerful enough to repel threats to our own shores and rally the Western civilization from which our country springs against threats powerful enough—and morally insidious enough—to destroy it.

Reasonable people can disagree about tactics but cannot deny the importance of confronting existential threats to civilization. Hitler was that. And we should not passively accept the decades-old, left-wing (literally Stalinist) propaganda that the Nazis were "conservatives." They were not guardians of free markets, tradition, or Christianity.

On the contrary, according to Hitler's chief architect, Albert Speer, Hitler said, "You see, it's been our misfortune to have the wrong religion. Why didn't we have the religion of the Japanese, who regard sacrifice for the Fatherland as the highest good? The Mohammedan religion too would have been more compatible to us than Christianity. Why did it have to be Christianity with its meekness and flabbiness?"[3] Speer not only emulated Hitler's brutal attitude and his warlike determination; Speer's thinking was the deadly opposite of every ideal we hold dear: civility, kindness, freedom, reverence for life, and the basic pragmatic concern for costs and benefits. To the maniacal semimystical leader, no tragedy was too much for his people to endure in pursuit of his vision. That's not our way.

In the short run, authoritarian societies appear to have a tactical advantage. They may pick one project, such as invading Poland or making the proverbial trains run on time, and for a short time succeed in seducing society's resources into the struggle. But eventually people notice the taxes they're required to pay, the regulations they're forced to comply with, the wounds they suffer, the loved ones they lose. Rest assured, authoritarianism is not sustainable in the long run. The trick is getting people to realize that sooner rather than later.

Make no mistake, war should always be a last resort. It was the pre-Christian warrior cultures and their latter-day imitators such as the Nazis and fascists who truly reveled in combat. But when the time comes to fight, we must do so with a clear sense of what we're fighting for. Once more, the fundamentals provide guidance in current crises. And British Prime Minister Neville Chamberlain, naively signing the 1938 pact to respect Germany's seizure of part of Czechoslovakia, remains a cautionary tale for the ages about the futility of appeasement.

Defending a Civilization

As the law professor Richard Epstein has said, there are few things more dangerous for the world as a whole than a US president projecting weakness and indecision. That doesn't mean the president should bomb everything in sight. Part of strength is forbearance, and there are usually means other than warfare of settling disputes. However, our allies and enemies are constantly watching us, sometimes testing us, to see whether we will back them or punish them accordingly.

It is important for the Pentagon to have some ability to predict its future funding levels. It is important for long-time allies such as the United Kingdom and Israel to know we still support them. And it is important for sometime enemies such as Iran to know exactly what behavior we will tolerate.

The final years of the Obama administration have repeatedly violated those precepts. In periodic budget impasses on Capitol Hill, the Pentagon has seen its budget held hostage along with all manner of other more trivial spending. The United Kingdom and Israel are both slightly farther from us than they were before the Obama presidency, perhaps because of Obama's Ivy League–style anti-imperialist, sometimes anti-Western philosophical orientation. Iran laughs at the spectacle of Secretary of State John Kerry declaring a historic antinuclear pact only to have the Iranian president state that Iran has signed no deal, would never sign such a deal, is accelerating its missile program, and will brook no pressure from the United States or violations of Iranian waters.

Make deals with dictators or don't, but don't pretend to do so and then make the United States look like a chump.

Unfortunately, the situation with the terrorist group ISIS also calls for steady and determined leadership that the country currently lacks. Are we bombing ISIS into oblivion, ignoring them because they're weak and trivial, funding their Syrian-rebel rivals, or at times funding ISIS factions themselves because we are solely focused on ousting Syrian president Bashar al-Assad? The complexity of the Muslim world is hardly of Obama's making, but it is arrogant and dangerous to pretend to have a handle on the situation.

Vacillation on the part of the United States starts to look worse than weakness and more like cynicism when the world hears that Vice President Biden's son and a friend of John Kerry's family are suddenly on the board of a Ukrainian gas company embroiled in the civil war there. Will that have no effect on the administration's foreign policy decisions? With the post-9/11 world being carved up by regional thugs and terrorist organizations, our main concern should be preventing World War III or more mass terror deaths, not seeking opportunities for crony capitalism and nepotism.

Critics will say that the defense industry is also made up of crony capitalists, big, powerful companies with lobbyists in Congress and long-standing ties to government. As an economist, I know very well that no Cabinet-level department is magically exempt from the laws of economics. There is waste in defense, as in any other part of government. But it would be complicated for the market alone to provide national defense, whereas markets seem to do a good job of providing housing, artwork, farms, and numerous other areas of the economy into which the government pokes its nose. We can decry waste, fraud, and abuse in defense spending without deluding ourselves that defense is unnecessary.

Yet when it comes time to try to make cuts in the federal budget—I say time to *try to make*, not time to *make*, since real cuts virtually never happen—it is almost always defense that faces the greatest pressure. I suspect the reason is twofold. First, defense is the only part of government, with the possible exception of the border patrol, that the Democrats don't fully love, so it's natural it would feel some extra pressure. But second, even with defense industry lobbyists, defense doesn't have quite the built-in constituency other parts of government do. You'll hear a ruckus from seniors if you make reckless changes to Social Security or Medicare. Artists and their friends in the wider media will speak up if you try to cut the National Endowment for the Arts. Hospitals and scientists will complain about (hypothetical) Department of Health and Human Services cuts.

Defense is more nearly a true "general welfare" program in the best sense of the phrase. As the Founders intended, that was not a catchall phrase permitting the government to do anything and everything it thought might produce some benefit to the public. Rather, the emphasis on *general* was supposed to mean that the federal government should spend only on projects that benefited every American and thus could not be done at the state, local, or private level, where nearly everything should be done. By definition, *national* defense affects us all. And when done intelligently, it benefits us all. As long as I'm in Congress, I will stick up for wise defense spending, even as I search for ways to trim bloat and overreach in countless parts of the federal leviathan.

Even during the second half of the 1990s, with Newt Gingrich in the Speaker's chair and Congress arguably in the most antigovernment, budget-cutting mood it had been in since big government began its steady expansion in the early twentieth century, almost all the "cuts" the so-called revolutionary Congress agreed on came from defense. It was not hard to do right after the collapse of the Soviet Union, our greatest international enemy. When the cutting starts, it tends to get as far as the Defense Department. Even with the big "peace dividend" that President Bill Clinton touted from post–Cold War cuts, only about 1 percent of the federal budget ended up getting trimmed,[4] and that restraint lasted about a year before things went back to their usual slow and steady expansion.

At times, the budget growth was even more rapid under George W. Bush. About the only reason budget growth has been slightly slower under Obama than Bush is that we've largely wound down the Iraq and Afghan wars. Thanks to the financial crisis of 2008, we're darn near broke or at least very deeply in debt. It's not a good time for wild new spending ideas. Think of that as a grim silver lining.

National Security Is Not a Blank Check

The staunch defense of liberty should not entail unnecessary restrictions on the liberty of innocent Americans, a distinction some politicians have a hard time making. We can frankly recognize the threat of ISIS or other terrorists striking within our borders, including "lone wolf" terrorists who take inspiration from ISIS, without being eager to spy on everyone's phone conversations and e-mails. A willingness to do that should not become the litmus test of the seriousness of one's commitment to national defense.

I have been critical of the National Security Agency collecting all Americans' electronic communications metadata, and the CIA has even spied on members of Congress, in part to learn about pending legislation. By any stretch of the imagination, that's a threat to the separation of powers, an executive-branch agency intruding upon the legislative process. If even Congress can't protect its privacy, what chance do private citizens have? Senator Dianne Feinstein (D-CA), who had in the past defended pretty much everything the intelligence community did—and all gun control proposals to boot—took notice once she realized her own Senate committee was being spied on. I can't say I blame her.

There have to be careful limits on this function of government, even in an era of heightened terrorist threats. After all, we must keep the threat in perspective. There were minor terrorist incidents in the United States almost monthly during the 1970s from sources including Puerto Rican and Palestinian radicals, who are rarely thought of as striking the US mainland in recent years.

I am not blasé about the present-day threat. In January 2016, two men accused of planning to join ISIS were arrested at Richmond International Airport, not far from where I live in northern Virginia. This sort of incident will be an ongoing part of our lives for a long time, but that is all the more reason we cannot fold up the Constitution and put it away at the first sign of adversity. The goal is to remain both alive and free.

Any resolution to the long-term war on terrorism, or at least a decrease in its intensity, may depend more on conflict resolution abroad than the sort of domestic security measures we deploy. While we argue about reading e-mails and tapping phones, important shifts in the balance of power in the Middle East may be occurring. I am certainly no Marxist (we'll revisit the devastating impact of Marxism in the next two chapters), but I recognize how often the philosophical and religious language people use to justify their actions is a gloss over economic conflicts.

As I write this, the price of oil has dipped, and Saudi Arabia, awash in oil money, is in danger of losing its position as head of OPEC. It has also experienced glimpses of domestic unrest, something an authoritarian monarchy is psychologically ill-equipped to handle. In late 2015, its execution of dozens of people for crimes including insulting the regime was likely meant to tamp down resistance, but it also had the effect of angering Iran, a traditional enemy of the Saudis. If we cozy up to Iran, it might in theory give us a stronger bargaining position in influencing an unstable Saudi Arabia.

We have a stake in influencing what happens in Saudi Arabia, in part because, despite being one of our primary allies in that region, that nation is also a prominent funder of Wahhabism, the radical Sunni Muslim creed that motivates all too many terrorists. An unstable Saudi Arabia could look much more dangerous than a stable but autocratic one, a dangerous calculation that Washington, DC, has been making for decades. Unfortunately, Saudi Arabia also recognizes that it has a stake in influencing *our* politics, and foreign oil money wields its indirect influence on many decisions in the nation's capital—as if home-grown influence peddling weren't a big enough problem all by itself.

It's Hard to Fight When You're Bankrupt

Half the battle in striking a strong defense posture is consistency. Just as moral rules erode if constant exceptions are made and market incentives dissolve if only some firms and individuals are given bailouts, we must be considered resolute by our enemies and reliable by our allies. Geopolitical circumstances and strategies change, but we can't let the world believe that the next budget shortfall in the United States could completely alter which nations we deem foes and which ones acceptable business partners.

If the military is overextended and we cannot afford to police some conflicts, we should admit it. If drone strikes or covert operations are more affordable than ground troops, the public can understand the trade-off, but we can't indulge in the pretense that a terror-supporting nation is now law-abiding just because we don't have the money to regard it any other way. A big factor in our cosmetic, quickly ignored nuclear weapons antiproliferation agreement with Iran—which at best has merely delayed its construction of nuclear missiles—was the realization that other nations were ending their sanctions against or lacked relations with Iran. Boom times might be coming with the United States left out in the cold, profits (and perhaps some new opportunities to wield business and intelligence influence there) forgone.

This is realpolitik and perhaps inevitable for a nation too deeply in debt to search for new wars to fight. But the spectacle of the United States continuing to talk as if it has the moral high ground and the will to fight in all such negotiations gets embarrassing at times. It's not just the influence of French-speaking Secretary of State Kerry that makes me think the emerging approach of doing business with authoritarian regimes while pretending they've met us halfway is rather French. Great as France is, it has never shown much aversion to doing business—including arms trading—with some rather nasty regimes, sometimes leading to our having to pick up the pieces later. How far the land of the crazed, guillotine-wielding idealists has fallen!

I have to hope that if the Obama administration, for whatever likely left-wing reasons, does things such as lift the long-standing embargo on still communist Cuba, it will, by accident or design, end up undermining the regime faster through commerce and contact between long-estranged family members than through more decades of periodic military threats. A willingness to trade backed up by the willingness to fight when necessary is a bit more convincing than a polite request to open a few restaurants or import-export hubs. But I well know the power of commerce, and in the end it's free markets we want, not conflict. In the next few years we will find out whether the rest of the world shares our desire for peace and trade, with Cuba and Iran being two pivotal tests, since we've taken the risky route of opening up to both after decades of blockade and sanctions.

Of course, fifty years ago, there was a wave of thought in the West that aimed to dispense with both military defense *and* commercial transactions. The left-wing project to undermine traditional Western values may have been at its peak in the 1960s, and it's that strange period to which we turn our attention next.

chapter ten

SAINT AUGUSTINE AND THE 1960s: THE FREE-RANGING FLUX OF CURIOSITY

I think freedom is naturally complemented by reason and morality. There has long been a perverse, false notion of freedom, though, that can undermine reason and morality themselves. That nihilistic impulse isn't new. Saint Augustine wrestled with it centuries ago. It is a thread of the Judeo-Christian tradition itself, gaining dominance in times of moral crisis, especially if the larger context of that tradition is forgotten. Popular culture did some forgetting in the 1960s, and, as we'll see, academics have been trying to bury some of our culture's memories for a long time now.

A sense of personal responsibility is a natural complement to a free-market society. Markets require individual property rights and the fulfillment of contracts. If you want to create a society dominated by government planning, it makes sense to weaken the sense of personal responsibility. The left has understood that for at least half a century. That's why the 1960s saw twin assaults on the market economy and the "bourgeois" virtues of thrift, self-discipline, modesty, and hard work.

If average Americans who want a more moral society vote for politicians who want to cut the federal budget, it's not because they're hard-hearted or harsh. It's because they sense how government's reckless spending makes good behavior seem pointless. The well-connected people are rewarded instead of the well behaved. If I accepted the ongoing waste and cronyism in Washington, I wouldn't be undermining only the economy; I'd be undermining American character. It's a very old struggle.

Alasdair MacIntyre has explained how different purported virtues are appropriate to different social settings, and the counterculture of the 1960s was an effort to remold society around its own chosen values. If you don't want to work, declare capitalism unjust. If you don't want to be sober, declare mind-altering substances the key to spiritual enlightenment. If, understandably, you don't want to get drafted, don't just insult the martial virtues or protest against ROTC—declare the entire capitalist system not worth defending against the USSR or the Vietcong.

This counterintuitive partnership between libertine and authoritarian thinking has deep roots in Western thought. It could almost be seen as reaching back to—and abusing—various aspects of the writing of Saint Augustine, who I promised earlier we would examine. He was the fifth-century Algerian bishop whose books *The Confessions* and *The City of God* (as opposed to the City of Man that was Rome) did so much to shape the thinking of the early Church. Modern thinkers of a decadent bent who wouldn't normally praise Christian thinkers nonetheless retain a soft spot in their hearts for Augustine because he admitted to leading a licentious and irresponsible life before coming to God. He didn't pretend he learned nothing from those early experiences, either, the "free-ranging flux of curiosity" eventually constrained by virtue. In that respect he is a precursor to the Romantic poets learning from loss and pain or the twentieth-century artist looking to the gutter for beauty, though all too many recent thinkers skip the coming to God part.

The deeper commonality between this fifth-century saint and the decadents of the twentieth century was the emphasis on a sphere of individual conscience, closely associated with freedom of choice. Much as Plato had emphasized finding truth in contemplation of the Forms, Augustine argued that an internal illumination was necessary to find truth. It may sound unsurprising to the modern reader, but that's because we have been steeped in thought influenced by Plato and Augustine's brand of Christianity for centuries. Without them, we might respond less readily to talk of individualism and the light of individual conscience and more to the talk of hierarchies and clans that dominates much of the rest of the globe.

Just as Plato thought that in theory each person had the potential to be guided by the light of reason, so, too, did Augustine write as though God saw a unique and important person in every individual. That is a powerful idea and a potentially revolutionary one in times of old-fashioned slavery or an all-controlling modern collectivist government. Augustine continues to project us along the individualist path that Charles Taylor saw as the natural, default trajectory of Western civilization across the centuries. According to MacIntyre, Augustine also steered the Christian tradition more toward Platonism (or Neoplatonism) than toward Aristotelianism in a few important respects.

As MacIntyre explains, Aristotle depicted individuals striving to embody various virtues and defined evil as merely a lack of those virtues. For instance, cowardice is the lack of courage, not so much a thing unto itself. Plato's emphasis was more on contemplation than on will. Evil, he felt, is a thing unto itself, and one is capable of choosing it, even delighting in it, not merely falling short in pursuit of some virtue. This is a slightly more disturbing picture of human life, but it rang true for Augustine, beset along life's road by myriad temptations. The Platonic contrast between shadows and Forms mapped easily onto Augustine's Christian contrast between materialism/hedonism and the life of spiritual discipline (one of many examples of Christianity open-mindedly borrowing conceptual frameworks from outside its own tradition).

Because of this tension, Augustine realized the potential to root arguments for both liberty and paternalism in Christianity. The individual should choose the good—life would have little meaning if he did not—but the occasions for sin will be many, and as a society we may desire to limit them. We may well have a duty, thought Augustine, to be intolerant of heresy. We may even be dangerously tempted by the desire to limit others' temptations, turning into authoritarians.

One way out of this dilemma, something of a cop-out, is to pretend that human desires can almost never steer us wrong. Another is to let the state make all decisions for us, so we can't err. Combine the two, and you have a formula for reconciling twentieth-century bohemianism with twentieth-century authoritarianism. What you don't have is much space left for the republican virtue discussed earlier: responsible individuals acting within a simple law code, engaging in self-governance and therefore in need of little external government.

For all his brilliance, Augustine is a mixed blessing, in part because he never fully resolved this tension between individual liberty and external authority.

Saint Thomas Aquinas, writing in the thirteenth century, had the advantage of drawing upon another eight hundred years of Catholic theology and post-Roman medieval legal theory, designed for a world in need of reliable contracts and courts and sometimes less stable than that of the ancient emperors.

Thomas did not treat the earthly realm of materialism and desire as wholly separate from the realm of contemplation and virtue, but rather asked how to bend or transform desire for moral ends. In this, he was very much a forerunner of the eighteenth-century Enlightenment mode of thought, taking certain physical impulses (almost like planetary motion) as givens and asking how best to harness, cope with, or alter them, even writing "Good is that to which desire tends."[1] Not surprisingly, he also endorsed private property, avoiding the antiproperty utopianism described in the writing of the English Catholic thinker Sir Thomas More two and a half centuries later.

Both the Greeks and the major Christian thinkers traced a picture of an enduring human nature defined as much by its flaws and shortcomings as by its possession of a divine spark. In the tradition of "natural theology" of which Thomas Aquinas was a founder, reason and faith are not seen as enemies. Instead, the experiences of the senses and everyday life affirm the claims of faith. There is reason to have faith, and the seeds of the humanist Renaissance are already contained in this medieval theology.

Compare this to the more brazenly mystical, transformational thinking of the hippie era. It would be convenient—and deceptively Christian-sounding—if indeed "all you need is love" or if you could "tune in, turn on, and drop out" without neglecting marital, academic, or business responsibilities. But it seems like a denial of the real world and the intractable human nature we use to navigate it.

Did Western Civilization Have to Go?

College students in the 1960s often regarded themselves as rebels against Western tradition, which had purportedly brought us nothing but racism, classism, sexism, and war. History was a chronicle of irrationality, and the current generation would transform themselves into better, more liberated creatures fit for a new and purer world. Even for this heretical view, thoughtful radicals might have looked back to our history for examples and guiding lights. But they chose to start from scratch, tossing out the baby of civilization with the bathwater of oppression.

Beginning with Stanford University in 1963, a succession of major universities has ceased to offer classic Western Civilization history courses to their undergraduates. In today's high schools, too, the grand narrative of Western ascent has fallen out of fashion. The reasoning was simple enough: if the West has had an outsize influence on the rest of the world since around 1500, it must be oppressive and bad; thus spending too much time detailing its achievements can only reinforce the remnants of that oppression. Better to junk the whole enterprise of Western civilization—and of course the Judeo-Christian tradition along with it—than to keep beating the drum for the bad guys.

But here's the thing: if the West has dominated the globe since 1500, and particularly since the nineteenth century, regardless of whether you think its preeminence has been deserved, that success stands in need of explanation. The political scientist Samuel Huntington coined the term "the Great Divergence" to refer to the way Europe and the West took off like a rocket economically after centuries of being merely one of several economic hubs comparable with China and India. Even to criticize the West, you must study its history. You will find slavery and oppression around the globe, so those things seem unlikely to be the crucial differentiating factor. On the contrary, it is the West's love of science, capitalism, freedom, and individual-respecting morality that seems to have done the trick.

I fear it is only by identifying the true causes of Western ascendancy that we can hope to estimate with any degree of accuracy the imminence of our decline and fall.

One of the great ironies of Western history, which makes the West hard to defend explicitly without being misunderstood by its critics, is that the glory of Western culture, the real mark of its superiority, is that it wasn't convinced of its superiority. The West borrowed. It imitated. Above all, it traded. And so it thrived, adding other cultures' knowledge and techniques to its own.

Similarly, religious and atheist activists alike risk misunderstanding Christianity's massive contribution to global culture if they think religion must mean a tough theocracy imposing its will on dissenters. You might say Christianity thrived because of its secularism. Religion can sap the power of the state, but too much involvement with the state can sap the vitality and hinder the development of religion.

Europe's path to the Scientific Revolution and the Enlightenment had its origins in the fundamental Christian tenet that church and state should be separate. "Render unto Caesar the things that are Caesar's, and unto God the things that are God's" is an injunction radically different from that in the Koran, which insists on the unity of any power structure based on Islam. It was Christ's distinction between the temporal and the spiritual, echoed in the fifth century by Augustine, that enabled successive European rulers to resist the political ambitions of the papacy in Rome.

Europe before 1500 was a vale of tears but not of ignorance. Much classical learning was rediscovered in the Renaissance, often thanks to the Muslim world. But a more decisive breakthrough was the advent of the Reformation and the ensuing fragmentation of Western Christianity after 1517, the year of Martin Luther's publication of the Ninety-five Theses. Rodney Stark argued in *The Triumph of Christianity* that ironically it was the defeat of central power in religion that would bring about its greatest success. He wrote, "The success of the West, including the rise of science, rested entirely on religious foundations, and the people who brought it about were devout Christians." The printing press and Martin Luther were the keys. The role of the modern "individual" was being formed. But as Niall Ferguson put it, "It remains undeniable that this was an intellectual revolution even more transformative than the religious revolution that preceded and unintentionally begat it."[2] The same communications revolution launched modern scientific inquiry.

However, noted Ferguson, the "principal concern of Enlightenment was not natural science but social science, which the Scottish philosopher David Hume called the science of man. . . . [T]he eighteenth-century philosophers were more concerned to propose how human society might be or ought to be."[3] Yet curiously, while the natural sciences continue to thrive—and economic and political sciences devised during the Enlightenment are still with us—the hoped-for One True Enlightenment Ethos does not appear to have emerged. The Judeo-Christian tradition is the only ethical game in town, and its intimate relationship with human reason is the key to our civilization enduring.

The Renaissance was another of Western civilization's mixed blessings. The turn toward humanism boosted the arts and sciences, but at the same time it unleashed superstitions not seen since ancient times, and quack remedies, cults, and prognosticators abounded. Likewise, freedom was in the air as pamphlets and manifestos quickly multiplied (a foretaste of our own era of blogs and Twitter), but unprecedentedly progovernment ideas such as "absolute" monarchy did too. As we will see in the next chapter, the Enlightenment would also prove to be a two-edged sword, with ideas both liberating and dangerous.

Throwing out Bathing with the Bathwater

The big mistake of the aptly named counterculture in the mid– to late twentieth century was believing it could judge the West's history only by its errors, as if the successes were common sense, to be taken for granted, as though they had not been forged by centuries of trial and error in the protective environment of a prevailing Judeo-Christian ethos. The counterculture's naïveté was much like that of a socialist who, glancing at the economy, concludes that a future socialist government will be able to preserve only the successful businesses without all the waste of unsuccessful ones.

Few hippies really wanted to do without basic moral rules such as doing unto others as you would have them do unto you, not stealing, not killing. Not to mention legal rules such as free-speech protections, due process for arrestees, and trial by jury. Those hard-won, proven methods of keeping the peace were the product of a discovery process and were spread along with the West's general prosperity. Yet even mainstream establishment political figures such as the Clintons tip their hats to the spirit of the 1960s, as if at long last a dumb civilization decided to do things right.

The left accepts at least one limited version of the thesis that the Judeo-Christian ethos was central to Western success, though: the late-nineteenth-/early twentieth-century sociologist Max Weber's notion of the Protestant work ethic. Beliefs shape behaviors— including those of efficiency and self-discipline—and those behaviors not only affect prosperity but shape cultural expectations about increasing well-being, the accruing of rewards to deserving and industrious parties, and which actions will be sanctioned by law.

A fuller understanding of economics and a fast-growing economy—but also a new assault on some of the traditions behind our success—would arrive with the wide-ranging intellectual inquiries of the Enlightenment, to which we turn our attention next. The ideas born of that era would end up saving more lives and slaughtering more innocents than any the West had yet produced.

In a sense, when a Republican presidential candidate such as Ted Cruz invokes the language of laissez-faire or constitutionalism and a Democratic candidate such as Bernie Sanders invokes democratic socialism, he is capturing the twin intellectual impulses born of the Enlightenment, still dueling today.

chapter eleven

ENLIGHTENMENT AND TOTALITARIANISM

T he eighteenth century saw the dawn of both free-market and socialist arguments.

Again and again in the liberal tradition—which, if defined broadly enough, includes modern American conservatism and all other philosophies rooted in individual rights, social contracts, and constitutionalism—we find arguments that have the potential to lead to freedom-respecting or freedom-denying conclusions, depending on subtly different interpretations.

The seventeenth-century English philosopher Thomas Hobbes embodied that dichotomy at a time of civil war among his countrymen. In works such as *Leviathan*, he responded to the risk of domestic chaos with ideas that were both protoliberal and authoritarian. As he saw it, men in the state of nature are in desperate need of having their rights protected—being spared constant threats to life and limb—but can secure those rights only by giving up all power to the magistrate, the Leviathan ruler whose word is law, almost an earthly god. Hobbes feared the alternative would be the perpetual war of all against all and lives "solitary, poor, nasty, brutish, and short." It is in one's own best interest, then, to submit to the king and rule of law.

In this, we can see a precursor to ideas such as social contract theory that would flower in more fully liberal fashion in the thinking of the late-seventeenth-century Locke and the writers of the eighteenth-century Enlightenment. In much the same way that Locke's quest for laws of political science has been likened to Newton's physics, Hobbes looked to the geometry of Euclid as a model for deducing eternal laws of political action. He ended up strongly affirming the powers of the sovereign, but he also raised the possibility that a sovereign, having a certain rational function and social purposes, could in theory be illegitimate. Hobbes became a controversial figure among both friends and critics of the monarchy.

It was as though Hobbes launched the modern inquiry into the rights of citizens by concluding that they don't really have any. The king was in charge, but new philosophical questions about his role were raised that echo down the ages to our own time.

Enlightened Ignoramuses?

One paradox of Enlightenment writers throughout the eighteenth century was their strong interest in human freedom and their enthusiasm to discover laws of human action that would enable them, much like the earlier Hobbes, to rationalize humanity's universal submission to the state. The mid-eighteenth-century French writer Claude-Adrien Helvétius argued that scientific analysis of humanity properly leads to measuring right and wrong in utilitarian terms, seeing all humans as equals, and rejecting the guidance of tradition and religion in favor of atheism. Like many political writers before our time, he ended up issuing retractions to avoid trouble with the authorities.

His recognition that the material world both constrains us and offers new possibilities for liberation in a way echoes the old concern of Augustine. There is a sphere for conscience but a world that continually deforms it. For Helvétius, science offered the possibility of transforming human nature—which began for the first time to throw all prior moral tradition into doubt, since it might no longer apply to remade humans. Yet the natural universe we are a part of was also deterministic: causal, predictable. Nature decides which political systems are workable and what desires will move human beings. The liberal tradition wrestles with those tensions even today, and philosophy students still fight over the question of free will versus determinism.

One of the greatest dangers of the Enlightenment's (well-intentioned) shift toward setting aside tradition and trying to discern the real laws of human action is that its thinkers—many of them in England, France, Switzerland, and Prussia—would discard everything substantive in morality to whittle it down to the rationally defensible parts. Helvétius believed that a radical reform of the educational system was possible only if political despotism and ecclesiastical obscurantism did not prevent it. In his frustration you can see an early version of the tension that exists even in our own day between radical educators, who would love to use schools to advance their progressive vision among children, and religious parents, who recoil from that or object that lesson plans ought to leave space for character education or mentions of the Bible.

In attempting to build a rational future, the Enlightenment risked throwing out all the lessons of the past that made the movement possible. The newly rising standard of living, aided by science and commerce, could be undermined if morality and traditional limits on the power of monarchs were tossed out as irrational. Recall

the French Revolution that occurred during this time, with rationality somehow leading inexorably to the bloody guillotine.

If the evil in human nature can be traced to specific causes,
according to Helvétius, what becomes of the dogma of original sin?
Indeed, if the causes of evil include the propagation of dogmas such
as the idea of original sin, what becomes of the whole theological
enterprise? This is the question posed most systematically by
Rousseau, whom we will revisit shortly.

The Scottish Enlightenment

Even at the time, figures such as the French writer Voltaire recognized that the English and Scottish branches of the loose
philosophical movement known as the Enlightenment tended to be
slightly less radical than the French and German. Voltaire admired
the English impulse toward toleration and was fortunate to live long
enough to see America and France moving in a republican direction
and the American Revolution beginning, but he didn't live to see the
French Revolution, with its descent into mass murder.

The Scots, traditionally said to be frugal, gave us, among other
thinkers, two of the most important economists of all time: Adam
Smith and, slightly before Smith rose to world-altering prominence,
his friend David Hume. Hume's wide-ranging interests have caused
him to be remembered more as a philosopher than specifically as
an economist, but he is a very important figure linking the long-
standing speculations about the human will in the Western
philosophical tradition to the rising discipline of economics, which
Hume saw as part of an attempt to create a full "science of man."

Hume largely severed rationality from desire, putting an end, as
it were, to the struggle that had been at the heart of Western moral
and theological thinking for two thousand years. For Hume, desires

were essentially nonrational; they were both arbitrary and a given for purposes of analysis. Rationality was the process not of asking what one should desire but rather of calculating how one might achieve it. For Hume, reason concerns the means rather than the ends. Indeed, it is the slave of the passions. Contrast that with Plato's imagery of reason as the charioteer guiding the yoked passions.

Significantly, Hume, influenced by fellow Scottish philosopher Francis Hutcheson (who had in turn been influenced by Locke), thought that moral judgments can never be truly rational judgments, since moral judgments plainly motivate action and no purely rational calculation can ever do that; only passions can. A split is introduced, then, between scientific, rational thought and all the psychological and moral moods that stir the heart. "Morality, therefore, is more properly felt than judged of," wrote Hume. "Take any action allowed to be vicious: willful murder, for instance. You never can find it, till you turn your reflection into your own breast and find a sentiment of disapprobation which arises in you towards this action. Here is a matter of fact; but it is the object of feeling, not of reason."[1]

With that turn in the mid–eighteenth century, Western thought began to sound less like the largely unchanging human nature questions I wrestled with in theology class and more like the strategic and pragmatic questions I wrestled with in economics classes. Hume was also an advocate of free trade, though he gets less credit than his friend Smith for it in today's popular estimation. He understood supply and demand and the deforming effects royal edicts could cause by interfering with them.

Like most modern economics writers who look at the movement of widgets without inquiring too deeply into character formation, Hume tended to take moral rules, such as the passions, as a given. He lived in times that were socially stable enough to regard the moral edicts of the day as fairly acceptable to all but disordered minds. The philosopher's or economist's job simply becomes figuring out how best to tweak those rules to facilitate the fulfillment of human desires.

To Hume's credit, he was not a fanatical moral or political system builder. He saw better than most how moral and political rules influence economics and thus human prosperity, but he also recognized the gulf between the ideal rule systems philosophers might applaud and the traditions humans actually live. In a rather conservative way, he understood that an entire tradition of moral rules, such as the Judeo-Christian, should not be uprooted to impose a new one. The real world will be an imperfect approximation of the philosopher's hopes—shadows rather than Forms, Plato might have said—but that is better than constant violent revolution or unrealistic expectations.

Hume even recognized, much as Alasdair MacIntyre, another Scot, would two centuries later, that traditions and moral context vary somewhat from time to time and place to place. But he was now armed with a rationalist's conviction that underlying economic laws—and certain unchanging aspects of human nature—meant that varying local customs would never stray too horribly far from functioning as facilitators of human desire. Even something as radical as a shift from monarchy to democracy could be seen as a mere adjustment of moral norms aimed at efficiency rather than a matter of extreme moral gravity. As he drily wrote, "Commerce, therefore, in my opinion, is apt to decay in absolute governments, not because it is there less secure, but because it is less honorable. By contrast, in the past, a subordination of ranks is absolutely necessary to the support of monarchy. Birth, titles, and place must be honored above industry and riches."[2]

Increasingly, the world made sense to Hume. The confidence that would later mark Whig and Progressive thinkers was being born, but first it took the form of laissez-faire.

A Separation of Religion and Academia

Of course, economics as such should know nothing about value-laden terms such as "progress" and "better," and certainly nothing about "salvation." How did they appear in economics class? A religious metaphor was smuggled into the core of economics and continues to reside there to the present day. The major schools of economic thought all follow the same logic and refuse to get their first principles straight.

Academia was not always this way, nor was economics always divorced from first principles and deeper foundations. In fact, wrote Robert H. Nelson in *Economics as Religion: From Samuelson to Chicago and Beyond*:

> It was appropriate that the American Economic Association was the first of the new social science professional associations. It was formed in 1885 as an outgrowth of efforts led by Richard Ely. . . .
>
> Ely was better known to the American public in the 1880s as a social gospeler, not an economist. He criticized religious leaders for their ambitious plans to reconstruct society that were not grounded in any adequate foundation of social knowledge. . . . If they shared with Ely the deep conviction that "Christianity is primarily concerned with

this world, and it is the mission of Christianity to bring
to pass the kingdom of righteousness," the application of
scientific methods to all the problems of society would be
necessary—from Taylor's studies of individual business
production methods to Ely's and other economists' studies
of the workings of economic forces more broadly.[3]

Therefore, the problems of economics were, as Ely put it, "religious subjects."

The economist Robert Samuelson followed in the footsteps of
John Maynard Keynes, as well as Richard Ely, John R. Commons,
Thorstein Veblen, and other progressive American economists.
Samuelson adapted the old progressive message to a newly scientific appearance, economics as physics. Many of the most powerful
forms of religion in the past three hundred years have been secular
religions that claimed the mantle of science. Economics was meant
to instill a religious commitment to the market and a commitment
to the priestly authority of economists to manage this marvelously
productive instrument for the general social benefit.

In this way, Samuelson sought to resolve the difficult ethical
problem of encouraging self-interested behavior in the marketplace
but excluding self-interest from the management of the market and
other key governing institutions of society. That is to say, he had
devised a new theological solution to the market paradox, one well
suited to his time.

So now we have economists in charge of the economic machine.
Self-interest is allowed to energize the system and provide the production needed for continued economic growth. But self-interest is
not allowed to operate in the realm of the centralized planners who
run the government. This is clever, but can it work? Has it worked?

Are elites self-interested? That depends on your religion, doesn't it?

The split between ethics and economics is important to understand. It likely goes back to the great eighteenth-century German philosopher Immanuel Kant, who argued that there are things we can "know" and things we cannot "know." Kant argued that we can't have direct knowledge of ideas such as God, justice, or ethics. In many ways, he created modernity. We can know things such as rocks and trees empirically. We can use our five senses to gain knowledge of those objects. The sciences were set up to study the realm of things that we can know for certain.

Economics emerged as a "social science" and has tried its best to fit into the "science" classification. Economists cannot see the "happiness" they want to maximize, but they can count the green dollar bills that make people happy. So we study the things we can count. Economics claims to be a science, and scientists have made it very clear that they do not do ethics. Science describes the world the way it *is*; ethics describes the world the way *ought to be*. This "is" versus "ought to be" language was famously emphasized by David Hume, who humorously discussed the problem in his work *A Treatise of Human Nature* (1739):

> In every system of morality, which I have hitherto met with,
> I have always remarked, that the author proceeds for some
> time in the ordinary ways of reasoning, and establishes the
> being of a God, or makes observations concerning human
> affairs; when all of a sudden I am surprised to find, that
> instead of the usual copulations of propositions, is, and is
> not, I meet with no proposition that is not connected with
> an ought, or an ought not. This change is imperceptible; but
> is however, of the last consequence. For as this ought, or

ought not, expresses some new relation or affirmation 'tis necessary that it shou'd be observ'd and explain'd; and at the same time that a reason should be given for what seems altogether inconceivable, how this new relation can be a deduction from others, which are entirely different from it.

Hume is correct. Many ethicists simply lay out facts such as "Millions of people go without food on a regular basis." This is a fact. Then the imperceptible move occurs to the "ought": we ought to do something about this. But by itself the fact that millions starve does not prove what we "ought" to do. Something else must provide the ethical argument. We must first say that starvation is bad, and we should give reasons. In other words, facts cannot get you to ethics. Many modern theorists want the data to speak in scientific fashion. They hope that the facts demand action, but they do not. Science has no ethics. Hume taught us the problem of "is" and "ought to be." Don't let the scientists act as though they have an answer to ethics. They do not. No lasting "Enlightenment ethics" has emerged.

Hume's cynicism was well founded and awoke Kant from his "dogmatic slumber."[4] Kant tried to answer Hume, but his answer would pose costs as well. One major cost is that we cannot "know" ethics or God in Kant. But what if faith is a firm and certain knowledge of God? At first those versions of reason and faith appear irreconcilable, and Kant is partly to blame for that immense historic split. Kant framed the modern conversation.

Economics lives in this modern world of Kant and therefore limits itself to describing the world as it is. No economist should engage in ethical claims—at least as an economist. Economists should make claims such as that the unemployment rate is 8 percent.

They should not go on to say that it is "too high." The latter claim would be normative or ethical. Yet of course economists do this all the time. Apparently, we were left unsatisfied by the constraints the Enlightenment placed on our claims and our professionalism, even as we celebrated the Enlightenment's clarity and objectivity.

I am an economics professor in higher education, and you may be surprised to learn the current state of the philosophical connection between economics and ethics in our discipline. There is none! I give a lot of talks on economics and tell folks that I try to connect economics and ethics. But the standard response is laughter. "Aren't you cute?" audiences seem to say. I remind them that their 401(k) plans are down significantly and that we likely lost a decade of economic growth due to a financial crisis that was caused primarily by colossal ethical failures. The subtext is: Do you still think it's funny for me to work on economics and ethics? Everyone gets it; economists and others have responsibilities.

Unleashing Wild Ideas

One danger of the Enlightenment's philosophical approach was that in its new lackadaisical or even hostile attitude toward tradition, it opened up new possibilities for increased efficiency but also for extremism. Unmoored from tradition, intellectuals are free to consider radical new ideas. They may not all be good ones, either.

The Enlightenment gave us insightful, moderate figures such as Hume, with his deep respect for property rights, but it also gave us the collectivist Rousseau, whose extremism influenced the totalitarian impulse in the French Revolution. The Enlightenment encouraged fresh and humane reflections on child rearing, the plight of the poor, and relations between the sexes. But it also unleashed the

Marquis de Sade, who wrote detailed descriptions of every violent sexual fantasy his uninhibited brain could conjure up.

Whereas the Continental manifestations of the Enlightenment frequently threatened world-altering, revolutionary consequences, the English and Scottish Enlightenment quietly made the world safe for science and free markets. By explaining more forcefully than ever why hampering markets reduces human welfare, Adam Smith cemented the modern role (for good or bad) of economists as formal or informal advisers to politicians, urging them not to impoverish their nations with ill-considered regulations. We fulfill that role still—when people will listen. Sometimes the public is underserved by economists who adopt more recent socialist views of the potential for regulation to improve upon free markets. On balance, though, I believe economists understand economics better than most people naive to the discipline. That's a low standard, but I think we can still do more good than harm, the classic utilitarian formulation.

Smith was the father of the modern assumption that the world tends toward a regime of unfettered commerce: global trade. He called this "true liberalism" of laissez-faire "the obvious and simple system of natural liberty."[5] I truly wish people still saw it as so simple and straightforward. Smith came from a Christian background (in an era heavily influenced by the minimalist creed called Deism) and had a philosophical sympathy for Stoicism. This combination—and not mere metaphor—led him to believe that a sort of "invisible hand"[6] would manifest itself in the efficient coordination of the marketplace if rulers stopped interfering with it. Contrary to many analysts of Smith who viewed his work *The Theory of Moral Sentiments* at odds with his more famous work *An Inquiry into the Nature and Causes of the Wealth of Nations*, I see in both the ongoing question—which the Stoics, Augustine, and Thomas Aquinas all examined—of how to turn human desire toward socially productive ends. It can be done through the profit motive, which rewards production, and reputation, which rewards good behavior.

The trust that freedom and prosperity were made possible by common sense and a rationally ordered cosmos is plainly akin to that felt on the opposite side of the Atlantic. The US Founders were interested in checks and balances and a properly limited government that would permit the people to engage in commerce and other projects of personal enrichment.

Adam Smith's Synthesis

The Stoic system of Epictetus seemingly drove Smith's system. But so did the Enlightenment philosophy of his day and the work of the moderate literati in Scotland; the philosophical systems of Hutcheson and Hume, which posit feeling and sentiment over rationality in the construction of morality; and the Calvinist system, which greatly shaped Scottish culture and education. The contradictions between these four impulses cannot easily be overcome, but Smith believed that the four elements did not necessarily conflict. He, like most Enlightenment philosophers, was a bit too optimistic about the new system he created. He thought he had found a new moral system that would transcend the role of traditional religion. That has not happened. The empirical data are clear on this.

In fact, Smith's system retains most of the fundamental features of the Judeo-Christian system. This is evident from his use of Christian terminology and his seamless transitions between Stoic and Christian virtues and between the gods of those two systems. When he is forced to choose between the two systems, his choices are interesting. On paper, he places Stoic reason above Christian revelation. But on the other hand, he chooses the Christian God over the Stoic

God. In the end, his choice of virtues and ends takes a decidedly Christian turn.

Smith's Enlightenment optimism also overrode basic Stoic doctrine. The Stoic universe was built on the assumption of an eternal recurrence of cycles in which no progress takes place. Smith's system departs from this cycle and enters the linear Christian cosmos, which is headed toward God and his causes and ends. Christianity begat progress.

Smith and the Enlightenment philosophers made a real contribution by teaching Christian theorists how much progress is possible in an environment in which reason can run free. So although the Christian system allows for this freedom and certain forms of progress, it took the work of Enlightenment idealists to help Christianity out of the late Middle Ages. Smith put reason above revelation. He was an Enlightenment Man. And he made the world more hospitable for Christian virtues. More often than not, a more prosperous world is a kinder one.

In our own partisan era we might say that Smith was from a red state because the culture and context that produced him were overwhelmingly Protestant. This context obviously shaped his education and thought. The elites and the institutions of his day were predominantly Protestant. Smith worked within these institutions. But was he literally Christian, let alone Protestant? In terms of his philosophical system and to some extent his moral system, the answer is a qualified yes. In terms of his own personal religion, one can only speculate. He believed that the universe is governed by a perfect, all-powerful, fatherly being whose ends are benevolence, justice, and love. Whether this is the Father of the Christian Trinity is not clear. The scholarly consensus at present is that this is probably not the case. It may well be that Smith was not certain on this matter. If there is a split in Smith, this is its primary philosophical source.

I further conclude that Calvinism trumps Stoicism in Smith's system. Though Smith would not agree, it appears in hindsight that the value added by Stoicism over the traditional Judeo-Christian system is hard to find. The reverse is not true. However, I admit that in the end, the influence of Smith's Christian mother seemed to fade, and the influence of his philosopher friend Hume increased.

Smith's system of economics and good teaching matters greatly because the father of modern economics knew that the world of thought must be unified. Positive analysis and normative analysis must meet. They do in Smith, and the ends of morality, economics, and jurisprudence are the same. However, in our economics textbooks, we act as if we are doing positive economic science, and we leave normative analysis for others with modern expertise. In fact, we are not doing positive science, and no one really comes around to clean up the normative mess we leave behind as economists. To get it right, we must go back to the father of economics, Adam Smith, the author who started from a unified moral and economic universe. We must recapture that synthesis.

If you are interested in further exploring how "bourgeois" morals helped build the modern economy, I refer you to the economist Deirdre McCloskey, who has written two volumes (out of a six-volume series) called *The Bourgeois Era*. In the second volume, she takes on all the Nobel Prize–winning economists on the topic of economic growth. Why did some countries become richer than others? Economists have proposed many answers, including capital accumulation, education, human capital, technological growth, population growth, the Industrial Revolution, trade, geography, modern science, and so on. But she examines those factors one by one and shows that although they were important, they were not the primary determinants of long-term economic growth.

According to McCloskey, the major determinant and primary cause of economic growth was the change in our moral language at about the time of Adam Smith when the businessperson and the entrepreneur became really "good." Business was a morally good calling, and that has made all the difference. If you reflect on history, you can see fairly easily that from Buddha to Hinduism to the Church Fathers, from Aristotle and Plato and the other Greeks to the Romans, business was depicted as something you put up with but do not necessarily admire. In the Renaissance, business was good to support your art collection and pay for things you wanted, but business itself was not considered intrinsically virtuous or morally good.

So there has since been a fundamental change whereby now the modern world—or at least many people, particularly in Western Europe—view business as a dignified profession and a goal for human life. And of course, when you think that what you do all day is morally good, it is motivational and inspiring. When you believe you can help other people, you will probably work harder and try to serve God and the world through your efforts on a daily basis.

The Seeds of Anticapitalism

Unfortunately, ideas radically at odds with Smith's tolerant and benign vision were also unleashed by the Enlightenment. Absent tradition, philosophers contemplated markets, but they also saw the potential for the state to rule over all, unfettered by either custom or commercialism, creating an ersatz heaven on Earth to replace the one they had lost faith in. Socialism was being born.

Throughout the subsequent nineteenth century, the post-Enlightenment world moved, in fits and starts, closer to laissez-faire than it had ever been before. The wealth and population of Europe tripled. Slavery was abolished. Constitutionalism restrained governments. Individualism and a relatively free press reigned. But the intellectuals were not satisfied with this unplanned environment. If the Enlightenment could make sense of the natural universe, should it not have dictated in detail a plan for regulated living?

The tragic fruit of that line of thinking was the regime in Russia that lasted from 1917 to 1989 and killed more human beings than any other form of human politics or philosophy, even Nazism. Impoverishing hundreds of millions of people, Communism followed a crude, authoritarian version of the nineteenth-century German philosopher Karl Marx's antiproperty vision. Incredibly, for all the devastation it wrought, socialism retains many followers among the intellectuals of the West, and in watered-down form it has a political defender in US senator Bernie Sanders.

As MacIntyre understood, one reason for Marxism's success in the West was that instead of presenting itself as mere authoritarianism, it could portray itself as the next logical step in the West's liberationist, Enlightenment, skeptical—even in some sense individualist—project. The most extreme version of the Marxist unraveling of older, traditionalist, Judeo-Christian assumptions in the twentieth-century and twenty-first-century academy has been deconstructionism, the largely French mode of literary and cultural criticism that treats all traditional knowledge as suspect because all knowledge claims are suspect (though Marxism, feminism, and quaint elements of Freudianism get a pass for being useful in subverting other modes of thought).

The deconstructionist critics most prominent in the late twentieth century, such as Jacques Derrida, represented a step beyond rationalist, antitraditionalist modernity into postmodernity. Such thinking has been an attack on *all* foundations and structures in thinking. God is out. Reason is out. Enlightenment projects are out. Science is out. Values and virtues are out. Jean-François Lyotard, a postmodern philosopher, suggested that for truth we substitute a new "language game," a celebration of ever-changing relationships among people and between people and the world. Without ethical criteria, you can see immediate trouble for these postmodern theories. Derrida criticized Western philosophy as privileging the concept of presence and logos, as opposed to absence. Richard Rorty argued that truth should not be about getting it right or representing reality; it is just part of a social practice and language that served our purposes in a particular time.

The postmodernists have no problem ripping systems apart and leaving *nothing* in place. These ideas—still espoused by thinkers such as Slavoj Žižek—are somewhat entertaining if you are into Nihilism and Nothingness. The postmodernists acknowledge that modern ethics has collapsed. They do have that right! Judeo-Christian ethics, science, and capitalism are the systems they worked so hard to collapse.

But reality has its revenge on the unbelievers. The attempt to run an economy based on Marxist principles collapsed in the Soviet Union in 1989 after decades of shortages and resource misallocations. Science keeps making discoveries even as culture critics denounce science's presumption. Deviations from free-market rules continue to yield economic failures.

Capitalism's critics create a lot of noise—sometimes understandably so—but take a look at the powerful signal behind all the noise: a recent chart of per capita income in thirty-five different countries taken from Dr. Daniel Gay and World Bank data.[7] Near the top are mostly free-market countries such as Switzerland, Singapore, and the United States. Below them are Western welfare states. Near the middle are former communist countries. Near the bottom are autocratic developing-world nations. See a powerful pattern? See the proof that free-market thinking isn't just rhetoric?

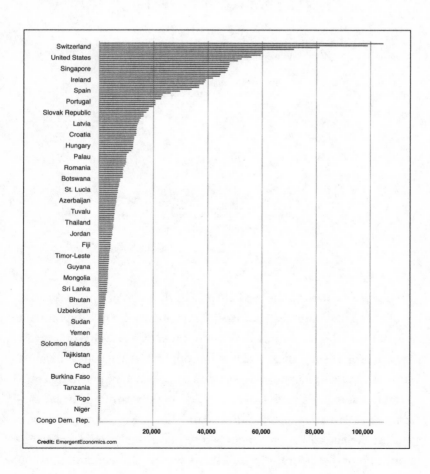

Credit: EmergentEconomics.com

The gains in income from living in a free-market environment don't all go to the rich. The next graph shows the incomes of the people in the bottom 10 percent of earners in four different groups of countries, from the least market oriented to the most free market. The poor fare better under capitalism.

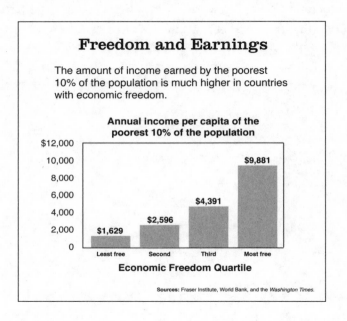

Freedom and Earnings

The amount of income earned by the poorest 10% of the population is much higher in countries with economic freedom.

Annual income per capita of the poorest 10% of the population

Economic Freedom Quartile

Least free: $1,629
Second: $2,596
Third: $4,391
Most free: $9,881

Sources: Fraser Institute, World Bank, and the *Washington Times*.

Before we turn in the next chapter to the current uncertain state of our own half-capitalist, half-socialist economy, I'd like to point out a final irony about the aimless postmodernist project. One of its most ardent proponents, the French philosopher Michel Foucault, most famous for writing about knowledge and prison systems being comparably controlling and sadistic, cycled rapidly through belief systems as varied as Maoism and Iranian Islamic Revolutionary fervor toward the end of his life. He hoped to make the larger deconstructionist point that no tradition, no stable system, is adequate or lasting.

But toward the very end, he became intrigued by one system that seemed to him to balance freedom and objectivity: neoliberalism, or what from a Marxist perspective might be seen as free-market capitalism. If the postmodernists are willing to follow their heroes all the way to the end of the road, they may yet loop back around to free markets and Western civilization. We'll welcome them with open arms.

But next, let's take a look at all the damage the anticapitalists have already done to our economy. With delusions of central planning dominant and talk spreading from Europe to the United States about the potential to stimulate more economic activity through negative interest rates, a reminder of what can go wrong in economics can't come a moment too soon.

chapter twelve

THE ECONOMIC
DEAD END

Bad ideas have bad consequences, and we're living with the consequences of bad economic ideas and policies right now, even as those keeping track of nothing but the Dow Jones numbers and the slight uptick in jobs numbers tell themselves that everything is back to normal and just fine. Among most citizens there is an uneasiness that hints at ongoing deeper problems. As I'll explain, though, economics is a tough discipline in which to bring up topics such as moral intuition.

To recap what we've learned so far: for us to believe in ethics, we also likely need to believe that there are good reasons for having them. We need human reason. If you think I need to give good reasons for this argument, you see the need for reason. And reason has resulted in many ethical schools of thought. The reason I have in mind started with Socrates in ancient Greece and extends to higher education today, but at present more cynics than true believers such as Socrates are on campus. Socrates did not claim certainty in ethics, but he did believe that the search for an ethical life is what makes life worth living. His student Plato was more willing to make truth claims regarding ethics. Plato's *Dialogues* are a must read, especially *The Republic*. In the Republic, both Socrates and Plato were more than ready to take on the cynics.

Today, most people are reluctant to make ethical claims of any sort, particularly in public. Just bite your tongue. So children are not taught about right and wrong. They are told that stealing or lying is "inappropriate"—whatever that means. My college students find it hard to commit to even the most basic ethical claims. Do you believe in human rights, women's rights, civil rights? "Well, yes, but that is just my view." That is really what they say these days. But we all surely know that rights claims are not only for oneself; they have to be for everyone.

If rights are trampled on by others, then we have no rights. If you think this can't happen in modernity, think of the Nazis. It has already happened. Rights disappeared overnight as a practice while the neglected truth of their existence was secretly unaltered. Why is the young generation hesitant to make ethical claims? Because in public education, our leaders are unwilling to claim that there are ethical criteria or rules we should follow. The tone at the top matters. The elites are tone deaf. So get ready for a dark new day, because if there are no ethics, there will eventually be no rights and no freedom.

For 2,400 years, the Judeo-Christian tradition and human reason were the main game in town when it came to ethics, but this is no longer true for public discourse. The Greeks had the initial burst or spark of reason, which then spread via the Catholic Church throughout Europe with a distinctly religious dimension. Saint Augustine and Saint Thomas Aquinas Christianized Plato, for example. The original virtues of wisdom, courage, prudence, and justice in Plato were eventually complemented by faith, hope, and love in Thomas and the Catholic tradition. The Protestants tweaked the Catholic system by focusing more on the individual and founding seminaries and universities throughout the New World.

Despite that long, interconnected tradition, it is now thought enlightened to dismiss our past or see it only as a source of guilt. On the left it has become a tradition to point to everything that goes wrong in the United States as evidence that "capitalism" has failed and we should abandon the values and laws that created this nation, hewing closer to the examples set by the more government-run economies of other nations.

Yet look at some of the nations most beloved by the left. Per capita income in China and India, the two most populous nations in the world, has gone from about $1,000 to $9,000 per capita per year.[1] Impressive growth, but it hasn't happened because of an upsurge in Marxism in those countries. In the mid-1980s, China's Communist Party chairman, Deng Xiaoping, introduced a subtle market, often by letting the Chinese military spin off private companies to cronies, which was not a perfect free market by any means, but a start compared to the days of starvation and mass murder under Mao Zedong's Cultural Revolution. The Tiananmen Square massacre of 1989 should be viewed as an attempt to slow down the forces of freedom that had been set in motion under Deng. Meanwhile, in India, a solidly democratic nation that had long voted for socialistic politicians, the embrace of globalization inspired domestic deregulation and wealth increased as never before, though incomes in that country still vary drastically.

Those countries were changing at the same time that communism was collapsing in Europe and the West's welfare-state assumptions were being seriously challenged for the first time in decades by British prime minister Margaret Thatcher and US president Ronald Reagan. What seemed like separate political developments then will probably be seen by history as a global shift in the direction of free markets. The socialist ideas that had begun percolating in the century after the Enlightenment were petering out.

But all that was a generation before the financial crisis of 2008. Now European nations are moving in a free-market direction while we're moving away from it. Having largely forgotten the moral and economic philosophies that account for its preeminence, the West was ill prepared to respond to the crisis with a return to fundamental free-market principles. With movements such as Occupy Wall Street making headlines and politicians repeating the old leftist claims about greedy bankers and insufficient regulation, you can't blame people for having a crisis of faith and thinking the anticapitalist left might have answers.

As I write this, the market remains shaky eight years after the September 2008 crash, and in the interim the solutions we've been offered have been born mostly of society's lack of faith in markets. The Wall Street–linked experts who have devised policy solutions have displayed the same socialistic, welfare-statist thinking that got us into the mess in the first place: easy money through ever-lower interest rates determined by the Federal Reserve, the governmental central bank, combined with bailouts for faltering firms and nearly a trillion dollars in miscellaneous federal spending projects. The left declares capitalism to be smoke and mirrors, and the pretend capitalists in New York and DC respond by creating more smoke and larger mirrors. That doesn't protect us from an even larger crash down the road. Only efficiency, increased production, and the paying off of debts can create a real expansion in wealth, the kind felt by our humblest fellow citizens instead of just a few well-positioned investors.

Despite some slow, painful growth, I still think the US economy is in trouble and our federal government is headed for a budget crisis. The Heritage Foundation policy analyst Justin Bogie notes five main reasons:[2]

- Spending continues to skyrocket. (We were already broke some time ago, and our strategy for coping is to pretend it's not happening.)
- Deficits will again rise to unsustainable levels. (We congratulate ourselves for making even the tiniest reduction in the deficit, but that's a far cry from having an actual balanced budget. Even that would not necessarily leave us far enough in the black to pay down the federal debt, which is the far larger problem—about $1 trillion a year versus $19 trillion with accumulating interest as far as the eye can see.)
- Our national debt will soon consume the economy.
- Increased revenues may increase the spending problem.
- A weak labor market is weighing down the economy. (A lack of new jobs, the phasing out of many old ones due to technology and uncertain future conditions, the mounting challenge of cheap foreign labor both beyond and within our borders, and the ever-growing tax and regulation on existing firms all combine to mean that many workers are giving up and exiting the labor market even as the government congratulates itself on slight improvements in the official jobless numbers.)

An Economy on Morphine

Frustratingly, from an economist's perspective, in just one generation our society has largely forgotten the most important economic lesson of the twentieth century: capitalism hauled billions of people out of poverty while socialism collapsed. The lesson was forgotten due to the bungling of the financial sector prior to the 2008 crisis and the faith placed in governments' central banks to provide the illusory fix both here and in Europe. Limiting government and allowing markets to function made us the wealthiest nation on Earth, and the record of real socialist regimes' failure is stark and demonstrable, yet anticapitalist populism is all the rage on both the left and the right.

During the twentieth century, the cruel trick that governments played on the public was presenting two models, neither of them a fully free market, to choose from: socialism, on the one hand, and on the other a heavily regulated and taxed system with a government-created central bank at its unstable heart, issuing government currency that since the early 1970s has not even been backed by something as reliable as gold. That has enabled government to print more currency—inevitably inflating prices—at will, fostering the illusion that economic activity is increasing even as goods become harder for ordinary citizens to afford.

Despite occasional stirrings of socialist sentiment among political activists and in creative and academic circles, the debate between centralized planning and markets in the broad sense is mainly over, won decisively by markets. However, subtler arguments continue concerning what can make the mixed economies we are left with thrive. The political class has a natural tendency to think that regulation and taxation are vital to society's success. A still subtler debate rages among economics professors—and now, with more urgency, among economic planners in government and industry—over whether massive downturns in the economy are natural, cyclical occurrences or evidence of deeper, ongoing systemic problems.

The strict free-market view, which I share, is that the inflation continually encouraged by central banks—through lower interest rates, easier access to new loans, the printing of more currency—produces a sort of hallucinatory euphoria. For a time, business increases and everyone becomes unnaturally optimistic. New projects are planned, new investments made, stock prices soar ever upward. But the crash arrives when people finally realize the euphoria was fueled in part by the mere creation of more paper, not by new inventions and increased worker productivity. Currency is not synonymous with wealth, and you can't create more of the latter—for very long—just by increasing the former.

Pity my fellow economics professors. They have become masters of economic statistics over the past century—they're understandably distrustful of anyone who doesn't have solid stats at hand—but the real engine of growth is hard to find in data. It's a regime of secure property rights and sound money, enabling business owners and consumers to make decisions—including long-term ones such as investment planning—with confidence. That's hard to do when the government might take part of your land next month or decrease the value of the dollars in your pocket next year. Uncertainty decreases risk taking, including the entrepreneurial risk taking needed for economic growth.

Yet both government and big business favor the continual inflation caused by central banks. As easy money flows into the economy, well-connected businesses and investors are more likely to be poised to take advantage of new loans, and government loves paying off its numerous debts with slightly less valuable bills than the ones that existed at the time of its initial contracts. The artificial boom-and-bust cycle helps those at the top—not only in government but also in business—at the expense of everyone else. No wonder there superficially appears to be a "bipartisan" consensus in favor of "wise" Federal Reserve micromanagement of the economy. It's mostly a matter of timing, with insiders more adept at acting upon their awareness of how the business cycle works.

It doesn't escape the notice of government that to some extent it can time booms and busts to influence voter optimism. The party in power tends to get voted back into office if easy money stimulates economic opportunity, and thus employment, right around election time. Not that such fine-tuning is simple to pull off. If the Fed could really turn knobs and alter things that easily, we would be living in a world in which central planning worked.

The Invisible Recovery

Consumers and small businesses aren't the only ones taken in by Fed-fueled short-term optimism. As I write, we are once again in a period of apparently increasing employment and a high Dow Jones Industrial Average. Analysts are making some optimistic long-term predictions. Yet the awareness of a potential crash seems to be growing in part because analysts have been making overoptimistic predictions for several years now.

That's not to say things haven't improved since the immediate aftermath of the 2008 crash, but they aren't getting better as fast as everyone kept hoping. Some of the reason is that the analysts, and no small number of businessmen, are themselves believers in the masterful stewardship of the government and the Fed. Even the ostensibly capitalist members of our society, stock watchers who would never call themselves socialists, tend to believe in the power of grand government projects such as Obama's "stimulus spending" when the alternative is despair.

We are told with ever-greater frequency that the Obama administration has guided the nation toward economic recovery. But it seems that Federal Reserve Board members and regional bank presidents keep lowering the standards for the economy's performance and continually revising their predictions for economic growth downward, from a giddy 4 percent in the second quarter of 2011 to a mere 2 percent in the third quarter of 2013.[3] It looks as though first-quarter growth in 2016 will have been below 1 percent.[4] No matter how bad things get, trust that we will be told it would have been far, far worse without whatever steps the president purportedly took on our behalf.

Afraid to accept the possibility that a Federal Reserve–guided, big-government-dominated economy is not as stable as they thought, the experts look to individual sectors of the stock market to blame for the ongoing cycle of booms and busts. Is it a natural rhythm? Is the housing market to blame? Admitting that the problem is far deeper and instability will continue moving from one sector to another risks people losing faith in the stock market altogether and giving up on investing.

Calling our current economic problems—the outcome of decades without sound money, with increasing regulation, without growing government—a "great recession" is actually dangerously optimistic. It misdiagnoses our current situation as a typical, cyclical downturn, implying that all we need to do to get out of it is wait, which suits Congress just fine, since making bold decisions and big reforms is virtually impossible now. Nothing is really changing on the legislative or regulatory fronts. That's bad news if we've broken the fundamental drivers of the economy.

Easy money from governmental central banks made government and private debt tempting and created a dangerously overleveraged financial world. In 2008 no lessons were learned, aside from finding out that if hedge funds and banks have enough of their former personnel in government, they stand a good chance of being bailed out when something goes horribly wrong (for the good of the system as a whole, they tell us, even as the system fails to reform or purge its bad actors). Media and regulators alike were terrified in 2008 when they saw how much debt investment banking firms had taken on. Naturally firms leveraged 40 to 1 couldn't expect to survive if their investments went south and they were left holding the bag. But the Federal Reserve and thus the taxpayer were left holding the bag instead, and the firms survived. Virtually no deleveraging has occurred since then.

After all, without accumulating debt, how could firms take more risky bets in the market? And so, in response to the 2008 crisis, we did little more than set ourselves up for the next one. Superficial new layers of regulation and accounting standards have helped to ensure that next time even more firms will make the same wrong moves at the same time, increasing the odds of a systemwide crash. Avoiding that outcome would require a massive, preemptive deleveraging. But there is no obvious way to achieve a colossal transfer of wealth from creditors to debtors without still more government intervention in the market, defaults, or inflation.

Shaky Present, Uncertain Future

If the United States has been experiencing an economic "recovery," it is a strange one. Consumer spending and confidence continue to be very low. The number of people who've stopped looking for work is high. It is as if the public senses the deeper problems the elites

refuse to address or have stopped believing reassurances from politicians and financial gurus, which may be wise. Even in the face of
politicians urging more economic activity, more short-term buying
and selling, the practical reason for the lack of consumer activity is
that people are busy paying down their household debts. They're taking a more realistic view of finances than the economic masterminds
who for decades distorted the housing and labor markets with artificially low interest rates and thought we'd never have to pay the piper.

It's embarrassing to have to admit that you won't be going shop-
ping for any luxuries for the next three years, but it's a more mature
and morally responsible reaction than anything we're seeing happen on Wall Street or in Washington. If current policies and Wall
Street practices do not change, our outlook fifty years from now will
be even grimmer than our current situation. If we currently lack
the political will to deal with trillion-dollar deficits and are suffering a lack of economic confidence with a $19 trillion debt, bringing
the growth rate down almost to zero, what will our country look
like decades from now, when it tries to pay down *$125 trillion* in
unfunded liabilities in the form of Medicaid, Medicare, and Social
Security payments?

One of the most heartbreaking things about seeing Americans suffer through the immense distortions in the market caused
by artificially low interest rates and government spending is that
people begin to think that all their old, good habits are irrelevant.
Being thrifty, working hard, and saving for a rainy day start to seem
like a formula for being duped. People aren't just being punished for
proper economic behavior; they are effectively being punished for
being moral. That is truly corrosive, making it that much harder for
the culture to embrace long-term decisions and refrain from indulg-
ing in some form of Hobbes's war of all against all—tax everything

in sight, become a well-connected crony, or just plain steal to get through the next week—as a strategy for survival.

Yet property rights and hard work remain—or should remain—the keys to personal financial success. Too often, people assume government spending equals reduction in poverty. But look at the government's track record. Poverty was rapidly decreasing in the United States *prior* to the government's so-called War on Poverty spending effort beginning in the 1960s. Right when that "war" began, the improvement stopped. Poverty rates leveled off. Compare that sad statistic to the improvement seen recently in Maine when it imposed a requirement for food stamp recipients to present their résumés in order to receive aid. People fled food stamps and welfare because it was easier to get a job than to keep jumping through the hoops imposed by the regulations. Good. They will be better off in the long run. Dependency on government is not the answer. It rarely is.

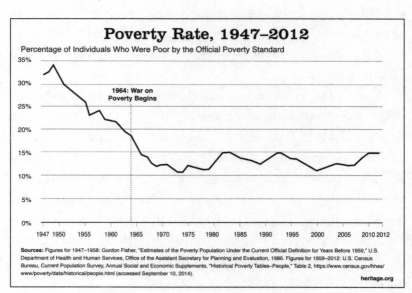

Poverty Rate, 1947–2012

Percentage of Individuals Who Were Poor by the Official Poverty Standard

1964: War on Poverty Begins

Sources: Figures for 1947–1958: Gordon Fisher, "Estimates of the Poverty Population Under the Current Official Definition for Years Before 1959," U.S. Department of Health and Human Services, Office of the Assistant Secretary for Planning and Evaluation, 1986. Figures for 1959–2012: U.S. Census Bureau, Current Population Survey, Annual Social and Economic Supplements, "Historical Poverty Tables–People," Table 2, https://www.census.gov/hhes/www/poverty/data/historical/people.html (accessed September 10, 2014).

heritage.org

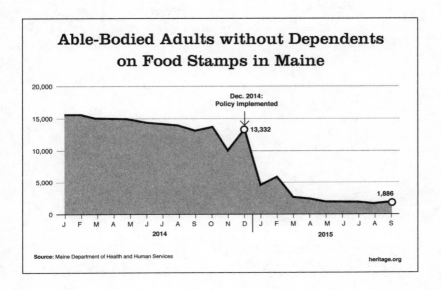

Able-Bodied Adults without Dependents on Food Stamps in Maine

Dec. 2014:
Policy implemented

13,332

1,886

2014

2015

Source: Maine Department of Health and Human Services

heritage.org

There is still a better way out of this mess, and it brings us back to the start. It is a freedom agenda based on our still sound ethical foundations, and we examine it in our concluding chapter.

chapter thirteen

THE ETHICS OF FREEDOM

For so long, elites have prided themselves on keeping their moral intuition (if any) separate from their "scientific" judgments about things such as economics. That's the opposite of what we should be doing. A conscious ethics of freedom may be just the thing to reunite our traditions, morals, and sound economic judgments.

The real wisdom in the Constitution is that it limits what government can do to us rather than limiting us to a few specific, residual freedoms. It's a moral document first, but it has big economic implications. If government were to define freedom and decide what freedoms we will have, we would be starting from much the same assumptions that economic central planners do: that power and knowledge lie with them, and we should be grateful to be part of the latest Five-Year Plan. (Or in the United States, perhaps it would be a Four-Year Plan.)

If, as the entire Judeo-Christian tradition leads us to believe, our rights come from God, the Constitution and our laws are just a recognition of already existing rights, a case of conforming government to moral reality instead of setting arbitrary new ground rules. A limited rather than all-pervading government is the perfect setting for a laissez-faire capitalist economy.

I mentioned Martin Luther King, Jr., in the introduction, and King can almost be seen as a final prophet in the great tradition that appeals more to freedom and freedom of conscience than to the desire to impose plans on society via the state. He may have inspired affirmative action programs and held some views conservatives will disagree with, but most people recognize that his real legacy was changing hearts and minds, a much more profound transformation than any set of regulations. America should still be able to summon the spirit of the individual to surmount social and economic problems. Our political vision should be undergirded by the assumption that we can act as free individuals to better our fate, not wait hopelessly to see what the policy makers will impose on us next.

I fear that Americans' confidence in individualism is waning and with it the aversion to central planning. Politicians such as the socialist senator Bernie Sanders strike a populist note by suggesting that recent economic troubles show that the rich are getting richer while the poor are getting poorer—that the left's worst fears about how markets play out are being proven correct. His answer, then, is to restrict markets through regulation, government spending, and more taxes to pay for it all.

Even if you're on the Budget Committee—it produces a ten-year balanced budget—I've learned that you don't end up shaping those "cromnibus"-type giant spending bills, cobbled together in semisecrecy by leadership, that the Senate and House vote on. Critics of us free-market-oriented politicians claim to fear shutdowns and radicalism, but the people seizing control of the budget process from the Budget Committee and Appropriations Committee are the ones behaving recklessly.

The truth is that the policies now failing in the United States aren't free-market ones, just as the much derided "austerity" policies of European governments aren't real belt tightening. Government is bigger than it has ever been, spending about 40 percent of Americans' annual income. The most deceptive element of this pseudo-capitalism is the increasing influence of the dollar-printing Federal Reserve over the stock market. Wall Street should constantly be on the lookout for well-run businesses and innovative products. Instead, its experts spend more and more time looking to the ebb and flow of the Fed's easy money supply to predict when and where to invest.

Originally meant to be only a lender of last resort and (in theory) to smooth out the business cycle, the Federal Reserve has become an endless money punch bowl. The distortions this causes in lending and investing inevitably favor big business and endlessly indebted big government (due to artificially low debt payments).

The result is an economy that might best be called delusional. Everyone knows the phony expansion is fueled by easy money and *must* end, but no one is really in a position to second-guess the Fed about when it *will* end. So we live in an unsettling twilight of ambiguous economic indicators—all the important economic data such as employment and productivity rates seemingly down yet the cheap-money-addled forecasts perpetually up—and manifestly wrong in retrospect for the past several years. The 2009 blue-chip consensus was wrong and much too optimistic. Despite all the happy talk, the Fed and regional banks continually revised their predictions for 2013 downward, starting in early 2011. Growth is now dipping below 1 percent and may hit zero.

We are in an ongoing financial crisis, not a mere recession, not even a "great recession." There is no painless way out of our situation, and we need to stop pretending there is.

That's why members of the congressional Freedom Caucus, such as Representative Jim Jordan (R-OH) and I, are willing to risk challenging status quo government, "barn-cleaning" and "crap sandwich" budgets, and even defunding unconstitutional provisions in Obama's overreaching agenda as long as the alternative is continuing to shirk responsibility until the inevitable economic collapse. So-called moderates who talk about "governing" as the alternative to taking principled stands fail to understand that the voters, such as the ones who elected me, fear that "governing" is code for saying yes to every spending proposal. If the moderates in leadership positions in government were honestly concerned about the United States' long-term economic health, they'd happily talk to the Freedom Caucus members when hammering out budgets. We could help them avoid the next mad scramble to avoid default.

Instead of government as usual, I say that we should proudly stand with every great, freedom-loving thinker in the Western tradition from James Madison to Martin Luther King, Jr., and proclaim an Ethics of Freedom to guide us through the current uncertainty as it has in past challenges. After millennia of humans living in violence and poverty, freedom is the source of our success, and we should be brave enough to stick to it. If we assume that the policy default is always in favor of leaving Americans free to shape their own lives and spend their own money, most of our political problems will be overcome.

The philosophy of freedom presents its adherents with different challenges in different eras—from slavery to Soviet communism—but a dozen political goals I'd like to see guide my fellow members of Congress as they craft policy in the early twenty-first century are these:

1. Remember that freedom is good for the economy.
2. Repeal Obamacare. Restore the doctor-patient relationship.
3. Rescue Social Security and Medicare through optional privatization and sensible cost-cutting measures.
4. Secure the border instead of subsidizing illegals.
5. Put term limits on the legislators who got us into this mess.
6. Oppose both No Child Left Behind and Common Core. (Education standards are declining despite those federal schemes, and the problem springs in part from no longer having a moral ethos in higher education.)
7. Audit the Fed.
8. Lower taxes to a globally competitive rate to bring businesses and jobs back to the United States.
9. Eliminate regulations.
10. Adopt a broad free-market energy approach.
11. Balance the budget.
12. And through it all, keep in mind the Tenth Amendment wisdom that decentralized solutions will likely be better than anything politicians come up with in Washington.

Already in my time in Congress, I've taken some steps to put these principles into action:

1. I voted to stop multiple bills that funded Obama's illegal amnesty and authored an amendment with Representative Mick Mulvaney (R-SC) to defund it.
2. I voted against the massive everything-but-the-kitchen-sink

$1.1 trillion cromnibus spending bill. Congress needs to learn to prioritize spending and show fiscal responsibility with your money, not just pass an all-encompassing spending bill hours before the deadline.

3. I voted against the misguided "doc fix" that increased Medicare spending without a way to pay for it. I want to see Medicare doctors reimbursed fairly for their work, but we need to find real cuts in other parts of the budget to pay for it.

4. I voted to deny President Obama fast-track authority on trade. It's a simple matter of trust.

5. I voted against the Iran Nuclear Agreement Review Act of 2015, which turned the Constitution on its head by watering down the two-thirds majority needed in the Senate to approve the Iran treaty to just one-third. Though the bill was well intentioned, people didn't do the math, and the act cleared the way for the recent bad deal with Iran. That's why I introduced HR 3199, an amendment to reinstate the constitutional guidelines for the Iran deal (which is really a treaty but called something else by the administration to bypass normal Senate ratification requirements).

6. I introduced an amendment that successfully stripped language sneaked into a defense bill that encouraged our military to recruit illegal immigrants. The recruitment push was especially insulting to our military because it was proposed at a time when we are laying off tens of thousands of US service members.

7. I continue to defend life by cosponsoring pro-life bills, including a bill to end abortions after twenty weeks (when science shows us babies in the womb can feel pain) and a

bill to keep Congress's promise to taxpayers ensuring no government funds go to organizations that provide abortion services.

8. I cosponsored the First Amendment Defense Act. When the Supreme Court declared that gay marriage was a right, it created a conflict with the rights of those who don't want to be forced to participate in a ceremony that is against their religious beliefs. The act would stop the Obama administration from punishing individuals, businesses, and religious institutions that don't want to participate in same-sex marriage ceremonies.

9. I introduced an amendment to the 21st Century Cures Act that would have stopped the creation of a new autopilot spending program. Though I supported the funding, I did not support taking it out of Congress's oversight and putting it on autopilot. Autopilot spending and interest on the debt will already consume all federal revenues by 2027, leaving nothing for defense, transportation, or other functions of government. This new program only adds to the problem. Though we had strong support, with 141 Republicans voting in favor, my amendment lost on the floor, with the rest of the GOP voting with the Democrats.

10. I introduced one of the simplest balanced budget amendments in Congress, designed for bipartisan appeal to increase its chances of passage, to get this country back on track economically.

We can get back on track while maintaining government's core function of defense. Indeed we can do so even more cheaply and less invasively if government doesn't police every aspect of our lives, including snooping on us via the NSA, IRS, and other arms of the booming surveillance state—and if we allow private citizens to remain armed, in keeping with their Second Amendment rights, which in truth are just a recognition of a more eternal right to self-defense that is innate, not created by government (check out www.davebrat.com to learn what else I'm working on).

I also recently introduced the Universal Savings Account Act with Senator Jeff Flake (R-AZ). This bill would let Americans have tax-free growth and save more of their income in a savings account. These accounts would empower Americans to save for any of life's events, such as education or retirement, and grow the economy by increasing funds for investments.

I introduced legislation with fellow freshman representative Seth Moulton (D-MA) to make all laws passed by Congress since 1789 available online in a modern, searchable format.

I cosponsored and voted for the A-PLUS Amendment to the Student Success Act, which would empower states by giving them the option to escape federal mandates and use federal education funding to focus on local needs and the vital connection between teachers and their students.

I led the charge against the end-of-year omnibus spending package that busted the budget caps previously put in place and funded the president's agenda through September 2016. This corrupt giveaway to K Street lobbyists was something I saw coming and warned about early on. Unfortunately, special-interest money was too powerful and our leadership gave up all leverage held by the GOP majority.

Sadly, while I was fighting the battles outlined above, Congress as a whole had different ideas. It passed a Medicare expansion that will increase the deficit by $141 billion,[1] created a new mandatory medical program that evades budget caps, suspended the debt limit, increased discretionary caps, and fiddled with the Highway Trust Fund without fixing its imbalances.

We Must Remember How We Got Here if We Are to Find the Path Forward

Policies don't arise in a vacuum; they tend to reflect a society's underlying beliefs. If we hew to individual rights and moral principles, our policies may in time come to reflect them again. If we abandon that ethos of freedom, well, we may coast safely for a little while. But if we do not remember how morals helped us succeed in the past and gave us the luxury to be so ignorant today, it will all end not with the heroic pronouncements of Nietzsche or a well-oiled (and imaginary) socialist utopia but with mere violence.

How can the left condemn the morality of capitalism when, since 1800, it has given common people standards of living like those of the kings of old? Prior to that, everyone on the globe lived on roughly five hundred dollars per person per year, which is now considered severe poverty. GDP per person charts leave no question that capitalist countries from America to Zimbabwe fare better. Capitalism is the compassionate route forward for humanity.

Morality and markets are not at odds. Adam Smith understood that stoicism, the Enlightenment, basic human sentiment, and Calvinism (or a Protestant work ethos) all contributed to the bourgeois ethic that makes our society hum. Alasdair MacIntyre's view that the West moves ever onward toward more individualism doesn't have to be pessimistic. Our history of individualism has been mainly an ascent, and we can climb to even greater heights of prosperity, freedom, and civility if we understand the principles that got us this far.

Freedom didn't happen by accident. It was not the natural state of humanity before the West's long climb. It was protected and nurtured by the Judeo-Christian ethos, which can shelter freedom even now. We must steer a path between people who advocate abandoning traditional morality and past restraints on the state and those, like some of our fiercest foes overseas, who say the state should be in the business of imposing a single religion on the populace.

Let's get right to the point. When Hitler marched through Europe, what moral foundation could have provided the language and power to stop him? What could overcome the combination of Hitler's National Socialism, Brownshirts, SS troops, propaganda ministries, PhD psychologists, German efficiency, and outright military dominance? The only moral force that could defeat that monster was the Judeo-Christian tradition.

The important thing to note is that when history moves against humanity, the truth is revealed. There was only one moral foundation available to do the job. There was only one moral foundation that had the language and the numbers to stop that evil. No other moral system appeared or even registered. Kant was the greatest German philosopher of the modern period, but his ethics rallied no one. Nobody used Kant's words. That is revealing. And it is a terrible revelation of the state of modern ethics because nothing has changed. In fact, we have lost ground since the World War II era.

What would happen if we faced a Hitler in our own time? What if, God forbid, a tragic financial or nuclear catastrophe destroyed our democratic system? What moral system could save us from such evil and enable us to rebuild? What language would be found? What could rally the nation to face the challenge? Ironically, the answer is the same as in Hitler's Germany: the Judeo-Christian tradition is the only moral system with the language and the institutions to do the job. The historical case is powerful, even if you don't believe the tradition's supernatural claims.

But could even the Judeo-Christian tradition succeed after the decades we have spent unraveling it? Have we prepared the next generation for such trials? Or is the tradition fading in power and relevance? No other tradition appears in sight, so it matters.

In response, some will say that a common morality exists across humanity that could accomplish the work. Other moral systems are possible. Of course they are. But did they emerge in Germany when needed? The answer is no. Where was this universal rational ethos of the human heart? Where was this core ethics that utopians dream of? It was not there. It is not here.

What language *did* emerge in civilization's time of crisis? What words moved people to sacrifice for their neighbor? In actual historical experience, it was the Judeo-Christian tradition.

This is not to discount good people or other traditions. It is simply to face reality. Many other traditions played a role for the good, but they were secondary, and they failed to halt massive destruction. That is the point. Do not let anyone past this major point.

When society asks what ethos can guide us through the current crisis, someone needs to provide an answer. My answer is this book. The deeper answer is the three pillars of the West with which I began this book: the Judeo-Christian tradition, the constitutional rule of law, and free markets.

The Freedom Caucus, by adhering to a version of those principles, has already been responsible for an increase in bottom-up talk of reform in the House, changes in the Steering Committee, the resolution of recent battles over the composition and tone of leadership, the promises made by Speaker Ryan to respect budget-trimming concerns (to which we'll keep fighting to hold him, as Politico, *Roll Call*, and others have chronicled). All those things were unheard of just two years ago. In early 2016, CNN said of the

Freedom Caucus, "They're the conservative group responsible for ousting House Speaker John Boehner and the ones who agitate for Republicans to hold firm on budgets. . . . They relish their reputation as king slayers even as they downplay their status as the House's new powerbrokers." *Roll Call* observed that in 2016, Senate Majority Leader "McConnell's goal was to begin a relationship with the Freedom Caucus leaders." A Politico headline proclaimed "GOP Field Courts House Freedom Caucus."[2]

That forty guys like me, Jim Jordan, and the rest, working together as the Freedom Caucus, can inspire these changes is reason for optimism. I'm hopeful that more and more people, both within and outside Congress, will join our cause, even as we learn to do a better job fighting for what we believe in.

Until then, I look forward to another year of keeping my promises.

Epilogue:
STEP 1, ARTICLE I

O ne of the first things Congress should do if it is going to take responsibility for America's current mess is take back from the executive branch the power it once had to address problems. As our faith in freedom has eroded, we have turned more and more frequently to the power of the executive branch—and presidents of varying levels of charisma—to play father figure to the nation and make everything right.

That's not the way the Founders wanted it to be, though.

I've joined a project of Senator Mike Lee and several of our Senate and House colleagues in something called the Article I Project, an attempt to restore the balance of power among the three branches of government—executive, judicial, and us in the legislature—as spelled out right there in Article I of the Constitution.

We hope to transform Congress's relationship to the rest of the sprawling federal bureaucracy in four key ways, by:

1. Taking back Congress's power of the purse, particularly putting an end to letting executive branch agencies call all

the shots by using continuing resolutions instead of real
budgets as spending guidelines;

2. Reforming legislative "cliffs," that is, threatening legislators
   with national disaster unless major fiscal bills are passed by
   an unavoidable but always nearly-missed deadline;

3. Restoring legislative control over regulations and regulators,
   since for too long most of the rules by which Americans
   live are arcane ones known only to a few bureaucrats in vast
   executive-branch agencies and barely even considered by
   the legislators who in theory make us a nation of laws; and

4. Reining in executive discretion, which has always allowed
   for executive orders and the like under understandable but
   unusual circumstances but has now become a way of life
   for a Washington culture that cheers for executive orders,
   so long as they come from a president aligned with one's
   preferred political party.

In short, what's the point of having a democratically elected
legislature if you don't use it? All three branches of the US government have contributed to our current dilemma, but Congress must
take primary responsibility for fixing it. Even as our entire republic drifts toward fiscal disaster, more and more of the government
has been put on autopilot, Congress barely weighing in except to
rubber-stamp, at the eleventh hour, budgets nearly identical to—
but slightly more expensive than—whatever budgets came before
them, with nearly all programs maintained at the same or slightly
higher levels of spending, regardless of changes out in the world,
including big changes in the level of anger and impatience among
the voters.

The larger the federal budget gets—now approximately $4 trillion—the less incentive each member of Congress feels to get his hands dirty trying to wrestle with any of the budget's endless details. It's easier to shrug, complain in public about the flaws in the process, and hope the system somehow holds together until the next fiscal cliff nears—and that if disaster ensues, the public will blame the other party more than your own. Instead of fixing small budget problems, we now lump them all into the macroproblem of the budget as a whole, then say that it's better to keep things as is than to risk fighting over the details or shutting the whole system down. We can't go on like this.

As Senator Lee describes it, the Article I Project has both a "horizontal" and a "vertical" component.

The vertical component is federalism, and it entails returning governance to the state and local level, where it was intended to be—even if some of the implications are ones a few conservatives may not like. Vermont, for example, might choose a very liberal approach to many issues that would, however, be consistent with the Constitution but not consistent with a law-and-order conservative's desire, say, to ban marijuana. On balance, it's better to err on the side of keeping the federal government's role in decision making—and spending—very small, though. More often than not, even if some crazy things happen at the local level, the locals will know what to do better than the Washington bureaucrats who are so tangled up in regulatory red tape, buried in spending bills, or teetering on the brink of the latest fiscal cliff.

The horizontal aspect of the Article I Project agenda is a reaffirmation of the separation of powers—the executive, the legislature, and the judiciary. Senator Lee advocates passage of the so-called

REINS Act, which would return relevance to Congress by mandating that all regulation with an estimated economic impact over $100 million be enacted into law by actual legislators, instead of put into place with the scratch of a regulatory bureaucrat's pen.

He also urges in his book *Our Lost Constitution: The Willful Subversion of America's Founding Document* that we remember five very important but "forgotten" planks of the Constitution:

- **The Origination Clause**: "All Bills for raising Revenue shall originate in the House of Representatives; but the Senate may propose or concur with Amendments as on other Bills."
- **The Legislative Powers Clause**: "All legislative Powers herein granted shall be vested in a Congress of the United States, which shall consist of a Senate and House of Representatives."
- **The Establishment Clause**: "Congress shall make no law respecting an establishment of religion."
- **The Fourth Amendment**: "The right of the people to be secure in their persons, houses, papers, and effects, against unreasonable searches and seizures, shall not be violated, and no warrants shall issue, but upon probable cause, supported by Oath or affirmation, and particularly describing the place to be searched, and the persons or things to be seized."
- **The Tenth Amendment**: "The powers not delegated to the United States by the Constitution, nor prohibited by it to the States, are reserved to the States respectively, or to the people."

At the same time, he notes the curious fact that although the parts of the Constitution clearly reining in the federal government tend to be forgotten by government (and political activists), the parts that can be interpreted to give the government broad latitude tend to be interpreted ever more broadly, the chief example in recent decades being:

- **The Commerce Clause**: "The Congress shall have Power . . . to regulate Commerce with foreign Nations, and among the several States, and with the Indian Tribes."

The commerce clause has been interpreted, in effect, to mean that anything that goes on in the domestic United States affecting anything else in the United States needs to be heavily regulated at the federal level. In the eyes of a government unmoored from its founding principles, "commerce" very quickly starts to look a lot like "socialism."

Just as this book was going to press, news broke that the federal government would forbid a potentially highly profitable and efficient merger between the US pharmaceutical giant Pfizer and the Irish company Allergan, largely because the feds want to squash any precedents for US companies using mergers overseas to decrease their domestic tax burdens. Think about that, though. Jobs will be lost, profits that might eventually have been used for expansion and for new lifesaving research will not be made, and a major US company will be stunted, all because the federal government thinks first of its own take.

You can describe that move by the regulators in terms that sound left-wing (socialism, anticorporatism) or that sound almost right-wing (economic nationalism, responsibility to the US Treasury), but what you can't argue is that it's consistent with Adam Smith or David Ricardo. They knew you have to let companies look around and seize opportunities for gains in efficiency, to find havens of competitive advantage. That will not happen if we crush every potential new combination of old factors of production. The Old West might not be the most efficient spot to make your wagon wheels anymore, and passing a law or regulation that says otherwise can't change that.

It's better to let people find new ways of doing things and let them get rich in the process.

JPMorgan Chase CEO Jamie Dimon said in the company's annual newsletter in April 2016 that the United States has a strong economy, "but we have serious issues that we need to address—even the United States does not have a divine right to success." Well put. Urging Americans to examine what parts of our overall system are working and which aren't, he went on to point out "some key concerns: the long-term fiscal and tax issues (driven mostly by healthcare and Social Security costs, as well as complex and poorly designed corporate and individual taxes), immigration, education (especially in inner city schools) and the need for good, long-term infrastructure plans."

He's trying to focus on that big picture that I mentioned in the preface. I'm not sure if we still can, at least not as long as we prefer petty political fights to our loftier founding principles and the timeless principles of a sound economy.

I know how hokey and old-fashioned it strikes some people to say we need to turn back to principles from the eighteenth century, not to mention from ancient Jerusalem or Greece, but consider the alternative. The modern drift toward expansive and runaway government hasn't made our society more "rational." On the contrary, it leaves us with absurdities like this list of a dozen sample areas of government overreach that Sen. Lee and the Article I Project identify:

- Treating even transient puddles as "navigable waterways" for purposes of Waters of the United States regulation.
- Making "recess appointments" of officials routine even though the Supreme Court has already struck them down save in times when Congress is not in session.
- Applying 1930s regulations to the Internet and calling the resulting stifling effects "Net neutrality" to make them sound cutting edge.
- Rewriting labor laws at a whim when requested to do so by union bosses, to the obvious benefit of Democrat fund-raising efforts.
- Pushing Common Core on the states, when just two generations ago we managed to educate kids without the federal government even being involved in education except in emergencies.
- Pressuring banks not to lend to disfavored businesses such as firearms makers and dealers via Operation Chokepoint—endless investigation without legislation, a chilling effect if ever there was one.
- Releasing Guantanamo detainees without notifying Congress.
- Using the Clean Air Act to regulate greenhouse gases after the cap-and-trade scheme failed to pass Congress—part of a dangerous "legislate or just do whatever the executive branch likes" pattern.
- IRS targeting of conservative groups for extra scrutiny.
- Endless wars without authorization from Congress, making even the hawks weary.
- And executive amnesty for illegal immigrants—even after the President himself said it was unconstitutional more than twenty times!

We can continue down the road that those examples show stretching before us: more arbitrary executive action, more government overreach, more expense without reflection, less regard for principles. Or we can wake up from our political and moral amnesia and hew once more to the constitutional, market, and moral rules that made the United States the great success story of the modern era. I can't determine which path we will take all by myself—nor should our system work that way. I can only hope enough of you share my desire to join the fight and rein in this leviathan.

Our government stands in need of drastic correction. Our underlying culture got a lot of very important things right. Let's use that to our advantage.

Our nation possesses an entrepreneurial spirit. Let us unleash that once more through common-sense reforms such as lowering our punishingly high corporate tax rate, which drives businesses to other locations around the globe.

Our nation possesses some sensible traditional ethical and legal rules, now at risk of being buried by an ever-growing mountain of regulations, created by executive branch agencies. Sen. Lee had his photo taken next to the 80,000 pages of the 2013 Federal Registry of regulations, which would stand eleven feet high if stacked. We should spend less time passing regulations, more time repealing them.

Our nation possesses a constitution well suited to guiding us through these problems, and in the very structure of that constitution is a hint that the executive branch was not meant to grow out of control. Article I of the Constitution, which describes the legislative branch, Congress, is three times as long as Article II, which describes the executive branch, the presidency. Our Founders expected a free people to govern themselves through their representatives in the legislature, not through a new monarch and the growing number of petty regulatory monarchs the executive branch produces. Congress must find the courage to govern responsibly again, not hand all authority over to the bureaucracy.

If we use these tools already at our disposal and trust them to guide us through our current crisis as they have guided us through past crises, we will thrive, winning against the odds. If we abandon our moral and political inheritance, we will face terrible consequences.

ENDNOTES

Introduction

1. Saint Augustine, *Confessions* (c. 397).

Chapter 1: Victory, or at Least a Start

1. Paul Steinhauser and Deirdre Walsh, "5 Aftershocks from Cantor's Stunning Upset Loss," CNN, June 12, 2014, http://www.cnn.com/2014/06/11/politics/cantor-loss-five-things/.

2. Dr. Eric Ostermeier, "Eric Cantor 1st House Majority Leader to Lose Renomination Bid in History," Smart Politics, June 10, 2014, http://editions.lib.umn.edu/smartpolitics/2014/06/10/eric-cantor-1st-house-majority/.

3. Alan Suderman, "Rep. Eric Cantor to Step Down Aug. 18," Associated Press, August 1, 2014, http://www.pbs.org/newshour/rundown/rep-eric-cantor-step-aug-18/.

4. Chris Cillizza, Twitter, June 10, 2014.

5. Jaime Fuller, "No One Saw Eric Cantor's Primary Loss Coming—in an Endless Number of Shocking Tweets," *Washington Post*, June 10, 2014, https://www.washingtonpost.com/news/the-fix/wp/2014/06/10/no-one-saw-eric-cantors-primary-loss-coming-in-an-endless-number-of-shocked-tweets/.

6. Kevin Cirilli, "Specter of Cantor Loss Haunts Republicans," The Hill, October 12, 2014, http://thehill.com/homenews/campaign/220467-specter-of-cantor-loss-haunts-republicans.

7. Laura Flint, "Comedy Central's Liberal Comedians Mock David Brat's Christianity," News Busters, June 12, 2014, http://www.newsbusters.org/blogs/laura-flint/2014/06/12/comedy-centrals-liberal-comedians-mock-dave-brats-christianity.

8. Shaun Kenney, "Slating Is Evil," Bearing Drift, March 10, 2014, http://
    bearingdrift.com/2014/03/10/slating-is-evil/.

9. Richard Billies, "What's All the Fuss about 'Slating' in Virginia?" Mr.
    Jefferson's Neighborhood, August 15, 2014, http://cvillelocalmarketing.
    com/historic-area-homes/.

10. Tom White, "Slating Thwarted in Henrico with Strong Grassroots
    Turnout. Cantor Suffers Significant Blow," Virginia Right!, March 24,
    2014, http://www.varight.com/opinion/slating-thwarted-in-henrico-with-
    strong-grassroots-turnout-cantor-suffers-significant-blow/.

11. Henrico County Republican Committee, "Official Committee Meeting
    Call," http://henricogop.com/wp-content/uploads/2015/04/2015-Henrico-
    Candidate-Night-4-20-15-Package.pdf.

12. Joel Skousen, "How the Republican Establishment Controls the
    Primaries," Liberty Roundtable, September 29, 2015, http://www.
    libertyroundtable.com/2015/09/29/how-the-republican-establishment-
    controls-the-primaries/.

13. Katie Pavlich, "Cantor Spent $168,637 on Steak Houses, Brat Spent
    $122,793 on Entire Campaign," Townhall.com, June 11, 2014, http://
    townhall.com/tipsheet/katiepavlich/2014/06/11/cantor-spent-168637-on-
    steak-houses-brat-spent-200000-on-entire-campaign-n1850194.

14. Julia Preston, "Republican Ideas on Immigration Could Legalize Up to
    6.5 Million, Study Says," New York Times, January 14, 2014, http://thelede.
    blogs.nytimes.com/2014/01/14/republican-ideas-on-immigration-could-
    legalize-up-to-6-5-million-study-says/?_r=0.

15. Charles M. Blow, "Still a Nation of Immigrants," New York Times, May 21,
    2014, http://www.nytimes.com/2014/05/22/opinion/blow-still-a-nation-
    of-immigrants.html.

16. Congressional Budget Office graphs are in the public domain. Other
    graph sources are cited within graphs.

17. The 2015 Annual Report of the Board of Trustees of the Federal Old-Age
    Survivors, July 22, 2015, https://www.ssa.gov/oact/tr/2015/tr2015.pdf.

18. 2015 Annual Report of the Boards of Trustees of the Federal Hospital
    Insurance and Federal Supplementary Medical Insurance Trust Funds,
    July 22, 2015, http://www.nasuad.org/sites/nasuad/files/Medicare%20
    Trustees%20Report.pdf.

19. "The U.S. Economy Slows to a Pace of 0.7 Percent in the 4th Quarter of
    2015," Washington Post, January 29, 2016, https://www.washingtonpost.
    com/news/wonk/wp/2016/01/29/u-s-to-release-figures-expecting-to-
    show-fourth-quarter-growth/.

20. Mark Thompson, "Draghi Poised to Give Europe Another $500 Billion Shot in the Arm," December 2, 2015, http://money.cnn.com/2015/12/02/news/economy/europe-ecb-stimulus/.

21. Tyler Cowen and Alex Tabarrok, *Modern Principles: Macroeconomics* (New York: Worth Publishers, 2011), p. 94.

Chapter 2: Why I Ran

1. Clyde Wayne Crews Jr., *Ten Thousand Commandments* (Washington, DC: Competitive Enterprise Institute, 2015).

2. Philip Bump, "The Story behind Obama and the National Debt, in 7 Charts," *Washington Post*, January 7, 2015, https://www.washingtonpost.com/news/the-fix/wp/2015/01/07/the-story-behind-obama-and-the-national-debt-in-7-charts/.

Chapter 3: Policy and Reality

1. "Recent US Federal Deficits by Year," http://www.usgovernmentspending.com/federal_deficit_chart.html.

2. Gary D. Halbert, "The National Debt Is over $18 Trillion, Not $13 Trillion," ValueWalk, July 5, 2015, http://www.valuewalk.com/2015/07/the-national-debt-is-over-18-trillion-not-13-trillion/.

3. Geoff Colvin, "Adm. Mike Mullen: Debt Is Still Biggest Threat to U.S. Security," *Fortune*, May 10, 2012, http://fortune.com/2012/05/10/adm-mike-mullen-debt-is-still-biggest-threat-to-u-s-security/.

4. Terence P. Jeffrey, "GOP: Our Budget 'Increases Spending at a More Manageable Rate'," March 18, 2015, http://www.cnsnews.com/commentary/terence-p-jeffrey/gop-our-budget-increases-spending-more-manageable-rate.

5. Jeffrey H. Anderson, "CBO: Obamacare to Cost $1.93 Trillion, Leave 30 Million Uninsured," *Weekly Standard*, July 27, 2012, http://www.weeklystandard.com/cbo-obamacare-to-cost-1.930-trillion-leave-30-million-uninsured/article/649066.

6. Paul Bedard, "Report: 21,000 Regulations So Far under Obama, 2,375 Set for 2015," *Washington Examiner*, December 31, 2014, http://www.washingtonexaminer.com/report-21000-regulations-so-far-under-obama-2375-set-for-2015/article/2558050.

7. Jamie Hennigan, "New NAM Study Shows Small Manufacturers Face More Than Three Times the Burden of the Average U.S. Business," National Association of Manufacturers, September 10, 2014, http://www.nam.org/

Newsroom/Press-Releases/2014/09/Pay-Up--Federal-Regulations-Cost-U-S--Economy-More-Than-$2-Trillion-Annually/.

8. U.S. Census Bureau, September 2014.

9. Andrew Soergel, "Where Are All the Workers?" *U.S. News & World Report*, July 16, 2015, http://www.usnews.com/news/the-report/articles/2015/07/16/unemployment-is-low-but-more-workers-are-leaving-the-workforce.

Chapter 5: A Tale of Two Revolutions

1. John Locke, *Second Treatise of Civil Government*, chap. 2, sec. 6 (1690).

2. Niall Ferguson, *Civilization: The West and the Rest* (New York: Penguin Books, 2012).

3. Edmund Burke, *Reflections on the Revolution in France* (1790).

4. Matthew Yglesias, "Emailgate Is a Political Problem for Hillary Clinton, but It Also Reveals Why She'd Be an Effective Leader," Vox, October 6, 2015, http://www.vox.com/2015/10/6/9461021/hillary-clinton-executive-power.

5. Alex Swoyer, "2015 Sets Regulation Record: Federal Register Hits All Time High 81,611 Pages," Breitbart, December 30, 2015, http://www.breitbart.com/big-government/2015/12/30/2015-sets-regulation-record-federal-register-hits-time-high-81611-pages/.

6. Frank Newport, "Congress' Job Approval at New Low of 10%," Gallup, February 8, 2012, http://www.gallup.com/poll/152528/congress-job-approval-new-low.aspx.

7. Tory Newmyer, "Hillary Clinton: Capitalism Is Out of Balance, Needs a Reset," *Fortune*, July 24, 2015, http://fortune.com/2015/07/24/hillary-says-capitalism-needs-a-reset/.

Chapter 6: Plato: Ideal Scenarios

1. Friedrich Nietzsche, *The Gay Science*, sec. 125 (1882).

2. George M. Marsden, *The Soul of the American University* (Oxford: Oxford University Press, 1996), 188.

3. Bernard Lewis, "The Roots of Muslim Rage," *The Atlantic*, September 1990, http://www.theatlantic.com/magazine/archive/1990/09/the-roots-of-muslim-rage/304643/.

4. Plato, *Theaetetus*, sec. 152a (c. 369 BC).

5. John Stuart Mill, *On Liberty*, chap. 3 (1859).

Chapter 7: Don't Do Everything as the Romans Did

1. Alasdair MacIntyre, *A Short History of Ethics* (South Bend, IN: University of Notre Dame Press, 1998).

2. Desiderius Erasmus, *The Handbook of the Christian Soldier* (1503).

3. Chris DeRose, *Founding Rivals: Madison vs. Monroe, the Bill of Rights, and the Election That Saved a Nation* (Washington, DC: Regnery History, 2011).

4. Niall Ferguson, *Civilization: The Six Killer Apps of Western Power* (New York: Penguin, 2012).

5. McIntyre, *A Short History of Ethics*, chap. 9.

6. Richard Hays, *The Moral Vision of the New Testament: Community, Cross, New Creation* (San Francisco: HarperSanFrancisco, 1996).

Chapter 8: Tribe, Nation, Empire, and Immigration

1. "US to Increase the Quota for H2-B Visas by 400%," Visa Reporter, December 19, 2015, https://www.visareporter.com/news-article/us-to-increase-the-quota-for-h-2b-visas-by-400/.

2. Edmund Burke, *Reflections on the Revolution in France* (1790), paras. 75–99.

Chapter 9: Not Just Playing Defense

1. Federal Budget Pie Charts, The Concord Coalition, http://www.concordcoalition.org/learn/budget/federal-budget-pie-charts.

2. Kathleen Curthoys, "Odierno: Readiness at Historically Low Levels," *Army Times*, April 2, 2015, http://www.armytimes.com/story/military/pentagon/2015/04/01/odierno-army-readiness-at-historically-low-levels/70805808/.

3. Albert Speer, *Inside the Third Reich* (New York, Macmillan, 1971).

4. Janet Hook, "House OKs Budget with More Tax, Cost Cutting," *Los Angeles Times*, June 6, 1998, http://articles.latimes.com/1998/jun/06/news/mn-57083.

Chapter 10: Saint Augustine and the 1960s: The Free-Ranging Flux of Curiosity

1. Thomas Aquinas, "Treatise on Law" in *Summa Theologica* (c. 1270).

2. Niall Ferguson, *Civilization: The Six Killer Apps of Western Power* (New York: Penguin, 2012).

3. Ibid.

Chapter 11: Enlightenment and Totalitarianism

1. David Hume, *A Treatise of Human Nature* (1738–40).

2. David Hume, *Essays and Treatises on Several Subjects* (1758).

3. Robert H. Nelson, *Economics as Religion: From Samuelson to Chicago and Beyond* (University Park, PA: The Pennsylvania State University Press), 41–2.

4. Immanuel Kant, *Prolegomena to Any Future Metaphysic* (1783).

5. Adam Smith, *An Inquiry into the Nature and Causes of the Wealth of Nations* (1776).

6. Smith, *The Theory of Moral Sentiments* (1759) and ibid.

7. Posted by Dr. Daniel Gay at Emergent Economics (www.emergenteconomics.com) from World Bank data.

Chapter 12: The Economic Dead End

1. George Magnus, *Uprising: Will Emerging Markets Shape or Shake the World Economy?* (Hoboken, NJ: 2010).

2. Justin Bogie, "5 Reasons Why America Is Headed to a Budget Crisis," The Daily Signal, January 19, 2016, http://dailysignal.com/2016/01/19/5-reasons-why-america-is-headed-to-a-budget-crisis/.

3. "Minutes of the Federal Open Market Committee, March 19–20, 2013," Board of Governors of the Federal Reserve System, https://www.federalreserve.gov/monetarypolicy/fomcminutes20130320.htm; "Economic Projections of Federal Reserve Board Members and Federal Reserve Bank Presidents, September 2013," https://www.federalreserve.gov/monetarypolicy/files/fomcprojtabl20130918.pdf.

4. Jeffrey Sparshott, "Weak Retail Sales in March Augur Ill for First-Quarter Growth," *Wall Street Journal*, April 13, 2016, http://www.wsj.com/articles/weak-retail-sales-in-march-augur-ill-for-first-quarter-growth-1460581888.

Chapter 13: The Ethics of Freedom

1. Howard Gleckman, "The Medicare 'Doc Fix' That Isn't," Tax Policy Center, March 26, 2015, http://www.taxpolicycenter.org/taxvox/medicare-doc-fix-isnt.

2. Lauren French, "GOP Field Courts House Freedom Caucus," Politico, February 16, 2016, http://www.politico.com/story/2016/02/house-freedom-caucus-gop-2016-endorsement-219331.